comparative public administration

public affairs and administration
(editor: James S. Bowman)
vol. 5

Garland reference library
of social science
(vol. 146)

the public affairs and administration
series: James S. Bowman, editor

comparative public administration an annotated bibliography

Mark W. Huddleston

Preface by Ferrel Heady

Garland Publishing, Inc. • New York & London
1984

Library of Congress Cataloging in Publication Data

Huddleston, Mark W.
  Comparative public administration.

  (Public affairs and administration ; vol. 5)
(Garland reference library of social science ; vol. 146)
  Includes indexes.
    1. Public administration—Bibliography. I. Title.
II. Series: Public affairs and administration series ; 5.
III. Series: Garland reference library of social science ;
v. 146.
Z7164.A2H8 1984 [JF1341] 016.35 82-49178
ISBN 0-8240-9182-5 (alk. paper)

Cover design by Laurence Walczak

Printed on acid-free, 250-year-life paper
Manufactured in the United States of America

contents

series foreword

The twentieth century has seen public administration come of age as a field of study and practice. This decade, in fact, marks the one hundredth anniversary of the profession. As a result of the dramatic growth in government, and the accompanying information explosion, many individuals—managers, academicians and their students, researchers—in organizations feel that they do not have ready access to important information. In an increasingly complex world, more and more people need published material to help solve problems.

The scope of the field and the lack of a comprehensive information system has frustrated users, disseminators, and generators of knowledge in public administration. While there have been some initiatives in recent years, the documentation and control of the literature have been generally neglected. Indeed, major gaps in the development of the literature, the bibliographic structure of the discipline, have evolved.

Garland Publishing, Inc., has inaugurated the present series as an authoritative guide to information sources in public administration. It seeks to consolidate the gains made in the growth and maturation of the profession.

The Series consists of three tiers:

1. core volumes keyed to the major subfields in public administration such as personnel management, public budgeting, and intergovernmental relations;
2. bibliographies focusing on substantive areas of administration such as community health; and
3. titles on topical issues in the profession.

Each book will be compiled by one or more specialists in the area. The authors—practitioners and scholars—are selected in open competition from across the country. They design their work to include an introductory essay, a wide variety of biblio-

graphic materials, and, where appropriate, an information resource section. Thus each contribution in the collection
provides a systematic basis for managers and researchers
to make informed judgments in the course of their work.
Since no single volume can adequately encompass such a
broad, interdisciplinary subject, the Series is intended as a
continuous project that will incorporate new bodies of literature as needed. The titles in preparation represent the initial
building blocks in an operating information system for public
affairs and administration. As an open-ended endeavor, it is
hoped that not only will the Series serve to summarize knowledge in the field but also will contribute to its advancement.

This collection of book-length bibliographies is the product
of considerable collaboration on the part of many people. Special appreciation is extended to the editors and staff of Garland Publishing, Inc., to the individual contributors in the Public
Affairs and Administration Series, and to the anonymous re-
viewers of each of the volumes. Inquiries should be made to
the Series Editor.

James S. Bowman
Tallahassee

preface

Bibliographic materials, essential for any field, are particularly important for comparative public administration, but they are also uncommonly difficult to assemble. Consensus is lacking both as to the central focus and the boundaries of the field, obliging the bibliographer to exercise considerable discretion as to what should be included and excluded. Whatever may be the choice as to coverage, the relevant literature is extensive, scattered, and diverse. Complete comprehensiveness is an impossible aim and would be unwieldy even if it could be accomplished. The bibliographer's task in comparative public administration is thus unusually demanding.

Mark Huddleston has responded admirably to these challenges and has produced a bibliography which has long been needed and will be used extensively. The most recent similar bibliography was published in 1960. Intervening bibliographical sources, although numerous and helpful, have been more limited or specialized in coverage. This bibliography includes some earlier items, but concentrates on the two decades from 1962 through 1981, thus providing an almost current guide to the most important published literature in comparative public administration.

The author is to be commended for being explicit and clear in informing the user as to the guidelines followed in compiling the bibliography. His most crucial choices are to define "comparative" as "non-American" for coverage purposes; to include only published items, mostly in the English language; to be deliberately selective, with emphasis on items found to be more significant, more recent, and concerned more with lesser-known regions and countries; to annotate each item selected; and to group the items by subject matter topics.

Although I concur with these criteria, not all users will.

Fortunately, the bibliography can be utilized readily by those who might have preferred other bases for organizing the materials. Huddleston provides an excellent user's guide in Chapter 1, builds helpful cross-reference systems into the body of the bibliography, and includes indices both of authors and of countries and geographical areas. These devices should enable the user to locate readily any item of interest contained in the bibliography.

Inevitably, of course, users of any selective bibliography will differ with the compiler on at least some of his decisions for inclusion or exclusion and on some judgments about the annotations. I, too, differ with him occasionally. My strong overall impression, however, is that we are in debt to Mark Huddleston for undertaking and bringing to successful completion a bibliography which is timely and praiseworthy. It will not wipe out the dilemmas, resolve the controversies, or assure the future well-being of comparative public administration, but it will contribute to our ability to cope with all of these concerns.

Ferrel Heady
University of New Mexico

the bibliography

PART I

USER'S GUIDE

CHAPTER 1

A USER'S GUIDE TO

COMPARATIVE PUBLIC ADMINISTRATION

This bibliography is designed as a research tool for those interested in the subject of comparative public administration. Strictly speaking, it is not a comprehensive bibliography, for not all items germane to this subject are included; given the tens of thousands of books and articles that touch on this field, true comprehensiveness would be unwieldy. Nonetheless, the more than six hundred references included in the bibliography offer full coverage of the major works in comparative public administration, and a fair sampling of virtually all topics throughout the world. Thus, even if one cannot find, for example, everything one wants to know about program budgeting in Nepal in the citations that follow, one can make a good start. The trick is in learning to use the bibliography to full advantage. The purpose of this User's Guide is to explain how to do that.

The Field of Comparative Public Administration

Before we begin, a few words about the field itself may be in order. To those with only a passing familiarity with the literature of comparative public administration, a bibliography on this subject at this time may seem peculiar. In recent years, articles have appeared in major journals of public administration announcing, if not always bemoaning, the demise of comparative public administration. After a period of great intellectual vigor during the 1960's, the field, it has been said, has quietly slipped from the scene. Peter Savage, one of comparative administration's foremost contributors, has ticked-off the absent vital signs:

The Journal of Comparative Administration
has gone. The Comparative Administration
Group has spent its half a million dollars
and has, to all intents and purposes, dis-
banded ... The Duke University Press series
in Comparative Administration has come to
an end ... Gone too are the fecund "summer
seminars," the easy assurance of panels
devoted to the field at professional meet-
ings, and the receptivity of scholarly
journals to articles in Comparative Administration. (item 27)

While all that Savage says is true, it would be
a mistake to assume that comparative public administration has indeed died. It is important to
make a distinction between comparative administration as a well-defined subfield of public administration and comparative administration as a subject
for academic inquiry. What has faded from center
stage is the subfield, or at least the most visible
accoutrements of the subfield, the grants and panels
and journals of which Savage spoke.

What has not faded, what is very much alive and
well, is comparative administration as a subject of
academic investigation. Research and writing on
personnel techniques, administrative behavior,
budgetary processes, and other dimensions of public
bureaucracies in non-American settings have been
voluminous in recent years, with the fruits of this
work appearing in a wide range of scholarly publications. It would not be far off the mark, in fact,
to suggest that the current level of activity is
outstripping even that of the mid- to late 1960's,
the period that Ferrel Heady has termed the "Heyday
of Comparative Public Administration." (item 8)
The difference now is that work in comparative
administration is not identified as such. Instead,
comparative analysis has begun to creep into the
substantive subfields of public administration. It
has not crept far enough to reach the mainstream
perhaps, nor have we yet seen Fred Riggs' prediction
that comparative administration will swallow the
rest of public administration (item 24) come to
pass, but we are on our way.

This is as it should be. All analytical endeavors, scientifically rigorous or not, are comparative endeavors. To say that one knows something
or understands its nature is to say that one has

recognized its special properties by comparing it
with other things, either in time or in space. The
more comparisons one makes, the more comfortably
one rests in one's knowledge. By the same token,
comparison is not an end in itself. Indeed, the
term "comparative public administration" must always
be understood as a shorthand for the clumsier but
more accurate "comparative study of public administration." Thus, however much they may miss the
excitement of the "heyday," veterans of the early
battles of comparative administration should feel a
sense of real accomplishment, for each step away
from distinctiveness for the sub-field has been a
step toward fullness for the field as a whole.

This fundamental optimism about the state of
comparison in the study of administration should
not be overstated, however. Several serious shortcomings in the literature, which have been recognized for many years, are still apparent. Perhaps
most troublesome is the fact that most research on
non-American administrative processes remains only
minimally comparative in the sense that single-
nation case studies are the norm, cross-national
studies the exception. While it is possible for
scholars undertaking secondary analyses to make
generalizations about administrative processes by
placing these pieces of research side-by-side,
aggregation is inhibited by a second problem again
of old vintage: data tends to be collected according to highly idiosyncratic frameworks. Now, however, it is clearer that conceptual disarray is
rooted not in the lack of a single comparative
administration framework, a chimera in any event,
but in the lack of substantive subfield frameworks.
A final problem, also a longstanding one, is the
relative paucity of empirical research in comparative administration. Any sort of comparative
fieldwork is difficult and expensive. It has become increasingly so in the public administration
field in recent years as cutbacks in American
foreign aid and technical assistance programs have
wiped out major sources of research support.

These problems must be seen as challenges,
rather than sources of despair. On balance,
comparative public administration is healthy, and
the prognosis is for continued growth. One way we
will know if it reaches its full potential will be
if in some future series of the Garland bibliog-

raphies the comparative volume disappears, and its
hundreds of entries become fully integrated into
the citations of the substantive fields of public
administration. In the meantime, this volume is
the place to look for material to assist the comparative study of public administration. It is to the
task of learning to use it that we now turn.

Coverage of Book

The first thing to learn about this bibliography is exactly what is and is not in it. More
precisely, since choices were made about which
references to include and which to exclude, it is
important to understand the decision rules that
were applied when the references were compiled and
annotated. Why did some items get in and others
not?

The first decision rule had to do with *publication*. Only those items published as books or articles were considered for inclusion. Unpublished
dissertations, manuscripts, convention papers, and
so forth were not reviewed. As with other decision
rules, this was applied not as a judgment on any
given piece of work or even on any type of scholarly
information dissemination, but rather in consideration of accessibility for those who use the bibliography.

A second and related decision rule had to do
with *language* of publication. In general, this is
an English language bibliography. Although this is
a limitation in a subject that intendedly deals
broadly with all areas of the world, it was assumed
that the users of this volume would be interested
almost exclusively in English language items.
Moreover, some significant exceptions not with-
standing, the preponderance of secondary material
of scholarly interest in this field is written in
English. The academic approach to public administration in Europe and in areas of the world subject to European academic influence is still
heavily oriented to what we in the Anglo-American
tradition would call public and administrative law,
and is thus not of prime interest to students of
comparative administration in this country. There
are exceptions, of course. Consequently, there is
a small number of references, annotated in English,
to items written in other languages, primarily

French and Spanish.

Date of publication formed the basis for the third decision rule. This bibliography consists primarily in items published in the past twenty years, from 1962 to 1981. The reason for going back only twenty years was simply that there is an excellent annotated bibliography in this field already in existence--Ferrel Heady and Sybil Stoke's *Comparative Public Administration: A Selective Annotated Bibliography*, 2nd. Ed. (Ann Arbor: Institute of Public Administration, University of Michigan, 1960)--and there was no reason to duplicate this work; nothing comparable has been done since that time, however. The date of publication of an item affected its likelihood of selection even within this twenty year period: the more recent an article or book, the more likely it was to be chosen. This rule was applied because, other things being equal, current information is more useful than dated information. Someone interested in a subject can go to a recent publication and by careful back-tracking through footnotes compile a full set of source material. This search process obviously does not work in the other direction. Publications that are widely considered classics, regardless of the currency of their information, have been included of course. This means that the intellectual quality of cited materials will, in the aggregate, be uneven across the twenty year period, a fact that should be borne in mind when using the bibliography.

The next decision rule, which concerns *geographical breadth*, introduces a similar bias. Generally speaking, the less that has been written about an area or country, the more likely an individual item about that area or country was to be included in the bibliography. For example, far greater selectivity was exercised concerning materials about Great Britain than those dealing with Malawi or Jamaica. In essence, the rule was, something about a country is better than nothing. Again, the logic here was that this at least provides the researcher with a starting point from which he or she can work back and identify other sources.

The final decision rule concerns the *substance* of the material. Any comparative items bearing on any of the following subfields of public administration were considered for inclusion: concepts and methods in administration; history of administration;

politics and administration; personnel administration; organization theory; budgeting; development
administration; local and field administration; and
citizens and administration. This rule is obviously
quite inclusive. Indeed, virtually any material
with a non-American administrative theme, with the
exception of administrative law narrowly defined,
was considered eligible for the bibliography. This
topical breakdown has also been used to organize
the chapters that structure the bibliography itself.

The completed set of annotated references was
produced by applying these decision rules to a large
pool of potential items. This pool was generated
by three principal search strategies: (1) a review
of other bibliographies in comparative administration and related fields; (2) a scrutiny of footnotes
in major works in the field; and (3) a systematic
survey of over seventy academic journals in comparative and public administration, related administrative sciences, political science, and area
studies. The complete list of journals searched
follows, items with asterisks denoting journals
likely to be of particular and continuing interest
to students of comparative public administration:

Administration and Society (formerly *Journal
of Comparative Administration*)*

Administrative Science Quarterly

African Affairs

African Studies

American Journal of Comparative Law

American Political Science Review

American Sociological Review

Anthropological Quarterly

Asian Profile

Asian Survey

American Journal of Political Science

British Journal of Political Science

Canadian Journal of African Studies

Canadian Journal of Political Science

Canadian Public Administration*

Canadian Slavic Studies

China Quarterly

Comparative Political Studies

Comparative Politics

Comparative Studies in Society and History

Development and Change

Economic Development and Cultural Change

Government and Opposition

Human Organization

Human Relations

Indian Journal of Public Administration*

International Journal of Middleeast Studies

International Journal of Politics

International Review of Administrative Sciences*

International Studies of Management and Organization

Japan Quarterly

Journal of Administration Overseas*

Journal of Asian and African Studies

Journal of Asian Studies

Comparative Public Administration

Journal of Commonwealth Political Studies

Journal of Developing Areas

Journal of Development Studies

Journal of International Affairs

Journal of Latin American Studies

Journal of Modern African Studies

Journal of Politics

Journal of Social History

Latin American Research Review

Management International Review

Middle Eastern Studies

Middle East Journal

Modern Asian Studies

New Zealand Journal of Public Administration*

Organization and Administrative Sciences

Pacific Affairs

Philippine Journal of Public Administration*

Policy Studies Journal

Political Quarterly

Political Studies

Politics

Public Administration (London)*

Public Administration (Sydney)*

Public Administration in Israel and Abroad*

Public Administration Review

Public Finance

Public Personnel Management

Public Personnel Review

Scandinavian Political Studies

Slavic Studies

Social and Economic Studies

Social Forces

Southeast Asia

Soviet Law and Government

Soviet Review

Soviet Studies

Studies in Comparative Communism

Studies in Comparative International Development

Western Political Quarterly

World Politics

In summary, then, the bibliography consists mainly in references to selected English language books and articles published from 1962 through 1981. As noted, there are slight biases in favor of publications of relatively recent vintage and of those which treat understudied areas of the world.

How to Use the Bibliography

Main Reference System

This book is divided into three parts. The
first consists in this User's Guide, which explains
how to use the bibliography. The third part, a set
of indices about which more will be said below, is
a tool to make the bibliographic material more
accessible. The heart of the bibliography is Part
II. Here the 624 references are arranged by topic
into nine separate chapters:

Chapter 2: Concepts and Paradigms of Compar-
ative Public Administration
Chapter 3: Administrative History
Chapter 4: Bureaucracy and Politics
Chapter 5: Personnel Administration
Chapter 6: Organizational Theory and Behavior
Chapter 7: Public Budgeting
Chapter 8: Development Administration
Chapter 9: Local and Field Administration
Chapter 10: Citizens and Administration

Each of the references is assigned a number,
from 1 through 624. These numbers are ordered
sequentially across the nine chapters. Thus, the
chapter on Concepts and Paradigms contains entries
1 to 34, the chapter on Administrative History contains 35 to 58, and so forth.
This system of topical organization should be
considered the main reference system of the bibliography. Depending on the research problem at hand,
one can turn to the appropriate chapter for an overview of the sources bearing on the topic.

Cross-Reference Systems and Indices

There are several cross-reference systems
built into the bibliography as well. These should
prove useful when more focused research questions
need to be addressed. To begin with, many items
are cross-referenced topically. That is to say, an
item may appear in more than one chapter if its
subject warrants. For instance, citation #404 concerns municipal budgeting. Consequently, it is
listed in the Budgeting chapter as well as the

Local and Field Administration chapter. To keep
things as uncomplicated as possible, however, each
reference has only one number, which it is assigned
according to its primary placement. Any further
(secondary) references, which also appear alpha-
betically, are abbreviated and denoted with asterisks, with the reader referred to the appropriate
number for the full citation and annotation. Since
in the example used above the article is mainly
about budgeting, the full citation for entry #404
has been placed in the Budgeting chapter; a secondary citation appears in the Local and Field administration chapter.

In addition to this cross-reference system,
some entries contain references to other items
that may be of interest to the researcher. For
instance, citation #394 is an article by Donna
Bahry on measuring expenditures in socialist countries. The annotation for this item refers the
reader to items 398 and 460, which are pieces that
respond to Bahry's argument. This method is also
applied to cited collections of readings. The
entry for the volume itself refers readers to
individual articles or essays that are annotated
separately.

Both these reference systems are built into
the body of the bibliography itself. An equally
important research tool is to be found in Part III,
which contains two separate indices. The first is
an index of authors, which is simply an alphabeti-
cal listing of all authors whose work has been
annotated, with the numbers of the entries associated with their names. This will be useful for
those seeking other work done by the same person,
either alone or in collaboration with others.

The second index is particularly important
given the special concerns of comparative public
administration. This is a country and geographical
area index. All citations have been coded for the
nation(s) or region(s) on which they are based.
Thus, if one is interested in the Sudan, for instance, one can look up that country in this index
and find that there are 4 references in the bib-
liography--numbers 138, 145, 146 and 185. One then
turns to the appropriate citations in Part II for
further information.

Conclusion

The comparative study of public administration is alive and well as an academic enterprise. Although comparative administration has faded as a self-conscious subfield, its spirit has pervaded and invigorated the rest of the discipline. All subfields of public administration--from budgeting and personnel administration to organization theory and behavior--have been enriched in recent years by increased scholarly recognition of the importance and utility of comparative analysis. The 624 references included in this volume were carefully chosen from among the thousands now available. This annotated bibliography provides an introduction to a growing literature for new students of public administration as well as a sophisticated research tool for experienced scholars.

PART II

REFERENCES

CHAPTER 2

CONCEPTS AND PARADIGMS OF COMPARATIVE

PUBLIC ADMINISTRATION

This chapter provides references to books and
articles that discuss theoretical approaches to the
study of comparative public administration. The
emphasis here is on methodology, and on the controversies and debates that have defined the conduct
of scholarship in the field. Because comparative
public administration has been an especially introspective enterprise, with its practitioners given
to examination and re-examination of assumptions
and theoretical frameworks, students new to the
field may find it helpful to read some of the conceptual overviews noted here before they attempt to
assimilate any of the substantive works cited in
later chapters. For this purpose, items 6, 8, 12
and 27 should prove particularly useful.

1.   Bendor, Jonathan. "A Theoretical Problem in
      Comparative Administration."
      Administration and Society, 8, 4 (February
      1977), 481-514.

      The central idea of "development" in compar-
      ative administration needs to be replaced with
      "evolution." The latter is more appropriate
      because it emphasizes random variation and
      natural selection, rather than determinism and
      unilinearity. Two problems with the evolu-
      tionary model are its difficulty to state in
      falsifiable terms and its relative lack of
      predictive power; these problems are surmount-
      able, however.

2.   Diamant, Alfred. "Bureaucracy and Administra-
     tion in Western Europe: A Case of Not-So-
     Benign Neglect." *Policy Studies Journal*, 1,
     3 (Spring 1973), 133-138.

     Basic thesis is that American political
     scientists, unlike their European counter-
     parts, have ignored the question of bureauc-
     racy and public administration in their stud-
     ies of West European politics. They have
     focused instead on politics narrowly con-
     strued--parties, elections, and so forth.
     Reviews American texts and American journals,
     assessing their contributions to comparative
     public administration.

3.   Diamant, Alfred. "The Bureaucratic Model:
     Max Weber Rejected, Rediscovered, Reformed."
     Papers in Comparative Public Administration,
     59-96. (item 9)

     Notes widespread dissatisfaction with Max
     Weber's model of bureaucracy, much of which
     is misplaced since Weber is too frequently
     read out of context. Examines Weber's
     writings on bureaucracy in the perspective of
     his typology of authority (*Herrschaft*). Pre-
     sents analysis of critics' views, most of whom
     charge that Weber was overly concerned with
     the formal dimensions of bureaucracy; this
     construction is based on too-narrow readings
     of Weber. More valid criticisms bear on
     Weber's relative inattention to the needs of
     bureaucrats themselves, the place of bureau-
     crats in the bureaucratic system, and tensions
     and inconsistencies within the ideal-type.
     The Weberian model is still useful for compar-
     ative analysis, although modifications are
     needed. The appearance of legal-rationality
     must not be confused with the reality.

4.   Esman, Milton J. "The Ecological Style in
     Comparative Administration." *Public
     Administration Review*, 27, 3 (September
     1967), 271-278.

Reviews Riggs's *Thailand: The Modernization of a Bureaucratic Polity* (item 521), Siffin's *The Thai Bureaucracy* (item 532), and Dang's *Vietnam: Politics and Public Administration* (item 79), all of which are characterized as "ecological" in approach. Although these are useful additions to the academic literature, they reflect a tradition that neglects the need for action-oriented, goal-directed theory.

5. Goodsell, Charles T. "The Program Variable in Comparative Administration: Postal Service." *International Review of Administrative Sciences*, 42, 1 (1976), 33-38.

Argues that programmatic content can level even large socio-cultural differences between bureaucracies, and thus provides an interesting focal point for study. Uses the example of postal services in the United States and Costa Rica to demonstrate point here. Suggests that this challenges the ecological perspective.

6. Heady, Ferrel. "Comparative Administration: A Sojourner's Outlook." *Public Administration Review*, 38, 4 (July/August 1978), 358-366.

Reviews past ten years of comparative public administration. Notes the general "introspective" mood of the field, and the decline of the 1960's "exuberance." Argues against looking for a common, consensual paradigm to revitalize study; instead, there is a need for new research strategies, and an acceptance of comparative public administration's role as something other than a distinct field confined within traditional national boundaries.

7. Heady, Ferrel. "Comparative Public Administration: Concerns and Priorities." *Papers in Comparative Public Administration*, 1-18. (item 9)

Introductory essay to item 9. Provides brief history of comparative administration field and discusses key issues of concepts and methodology.

8. Heady, Ferrel. *Public Administration: A Comparative Perspective*, 2nd Ed., Revised. New York: Marcel Dekker, Inc., 1979.

    Leading textbook in comparative public administration. Uses bureaucracy as a focal point for comparative analysis of Western, communist, and developing administrative systems. Although synthetic in character, provides excellent overview of specific national bureaucracies. Develops and applies a typology of "bureaucratic-prominent" and "party-prominent" systems.

9. Heady, Ferrel and Sybil L. Stokes. *Papers in Comparative Public Administration*. Ann Arbor: Institute of Public Administration, University of Michigan, 1962.

    Contains items 3, 7, 23.

10. Heaphey, James. "Comparative Public Administration: Big Science Model for the Future." *Public Administration Review*, 28, 3 (May/June 1968), 242-249.

    Assesses state of comparative public administration as of 1968. Identifies the main themes as "academic analysis" (Riggs), quantitative data gathering (Banks and Textor), comparative values and practices (Brian Chapman), and action-oriented theory (Esman). Argues that the relationship between these four visions ought to be viewed as the field's analogue of the complementarity principle in physics.

11. Heaphey, James. "The Philosophical Assumptions of Inquiry in Comparative Administration:

Some Introductory Comments." *Journal of Comparative Administration*, 1, 2 (August 1969), 133-139.

Reviews conceptual models used in comparative administration. Notes Riggs's concern with empirical theory rather than prescription, though doubts that distinction can be maintained. Moreover, there is a danger that the terms of reference for conceptual models (the "administrative reality" being described) are in fact dependent on the model itself.

12. Henderson, Keith. "Comparative Public Administration: The Identity Crisis." *Journal of Comparative Administration*, 1, 1 (May 1969), 65-85.

Overview of comparative administration literature and its relationships to American public administration. Begins with the work of the Public Administration Clearing House and the Comparative Administration Group. Concludes with projections as to likely developments in comparative administration. Predicts and is concerned about increased split between academics and practitioners.

13. Hopkins, Jack W. "Contemporary Research on Public Administration and Bureaucracies in Latin America." *Latin American Research Review*, IX, 1 (Spring 1974), 109-139.

Surveys research on administration in Latin America. Includes mainly books and articles in English. Categorizes into: (1) broadly theoretical; (2) new data; (3) development-oriented. Does not evaluate quality of work.

* Hough, Jerry F. "The Bureaucratic Model and the Nature of the Soviet System." Cited as item 359.

14. Ilchman, Warren. *Comparative Public Administration and 'Conventional Wisdom.'* Beverly Hills and London: Sage, 1971.

Critical intellectual history of comparative public administration and especially of the contributions of members of the Comparative Administration Group. Reviews and synthesizes research on what he identifies as five central questions preoccupying scholars of comparative administration, dealing with power, productivity, organizational form, roles, and system maintenance.

15. Jackson, Robert H. "An Analysis of the Comparative Public Administration Movement." *Canadian Public Administration*, 9, 1 (March 1966), 108-130.

Analyzes the sources, assumptions, methodologies and accomplishments of the comparative administration movement. Concludes that the major result has been in the area of model-building, in response to search for "culture free" analysis. While this has injected an emphasis on rigor into public administration, a preoccupation with conceptual problems has been detrimental. Too few empirical applications have been forthcoming.

16. Jreisat, Jamil E. "Synthesis and Relevance in Comparative Public Administration." *Public Administration Review*, 35, 6 (November/December 1975), 663-671.

General review and critique of the comparative administration movement. Argues that "middle range theory"--at the level of institutions rather than whole national systems--will produce greater theoretical relevance and synthesis.

17. Jun, Jong S. "Renewing the Study of Comparative Administration: Some Reflections on the Current Possibilities." *Public*

Administration Review, 36, 6 (November/
December 1976), 641-647.

There are two major lines of development for
comparative public administration: (a) acceptance of theoretical diversity or (b) adoption
of phenomenological perspective as a way of
integrating theory. Topics in the field that
need to be revitalized include bureaucratiza-
tion/de-bureaucratization, development administration, organization theory, and self-
management.

18. Landau, Martin. "Decision Theory and Compara-
     tive Public Administration." *Comparative
     Political Studies*, 1, 2 (July 1968), 175-
     196.

     Administration must be considered the inde-
     pendent variable in an hypothesis of change,
     for it is designed to transform one state of
     affairs to another. Comparative analysis is
     an essential part of "testing" this hypothesis.
     Discusses problems involved in studying politi-
     cal and administrative development. Views
     culture as a decision system, and using a
     2 X 2 table, outlines four types of decisions
     given social agreement on causation and
     preferences.

*   Loveman, Brian. "The Comparative Administra-
     tion Group, Development Administration and
     Antidevelopment." Cited as item 502.

19. Miller, Robert F. "The New Science of Ad-
     ministration in the U.S.S.R." *Administra-
     tive Science Quarterly*, 16, 3 (September
     1971), 247-257.

     Reviews recent Soviet literature in public
     administration and organization theory. Notes
     revival in administrative science in post-
     Stalin era. Although many concepts are
     borrowed from the West, they are usually
     applied with distinctive twists. These

developments have provoked a reaction from
some party members who wish to preserve the
purity of Marxist social theory.

20. Milne, R.S. "Comparisons and Models in
     Public Administration." *Political Studies*,
     X, 1 (February 1962), 1-14.

     Reviews Fred Riggs's work, particularly his
     Agraria and Industria models. Comments on
     appropriate directions for model construction
     in comparative administration.

21. Raphaeli, Nimrod, ed. *Readings in Comparative
     Public Administration*. Boston: Allyn and
     Bacon, 1967.

     Compendium of thirty reprinted articles,
     with a short nonannotated bibliography.

22. Riggs, Fred W. "Bureaucratic Politics in
     Comparative Perspective." *Journal of
     Comparative Administration*, 1, 1 (May 1969),
     5-38.

     A plea for clearer concepts, and theories
     that move beyond an obsession with the politi-
     cal roles of bureaucrats is followed by an
     analytical model. Political systems, accord-
     ing to this model, consist of two parts: a
     bureaucracy and constitutive elements. The
     relationship between these parts may be
     "balanced" or "unbalanced." Governments are
     more likely to carry out successful develop-
     ment programs if they are balanced. Hence,
     unbalanced polities should be transformed into
     balanced polities.

23. Riggs, Fred W. "An Ecological Approach: The
     'Sala' Model." *Papers in Comparative Public
     Administration*, 19-36. (item 9)

     Argues that there is a need for a model of
     administrative systems tailored to the

developing world. Offers the "sala model," which is the administrative component of "prismatic societies." The sala is characterized by nepotism, "poly-communalism," "poly-normativism," and overlapping authority. Emphasis throughout on "ecological" relationships--the ties between an administrative system and its surrounding socioeconomic context. Bureaucratic structures and behaviors are chiefly a product of their ecological setting. Concludes by suggesting that the sala model and the prismatic framework provide the basis for the development of general hypotheses in comparative administration.

24. Riggs, Fred W. "The Group and the Movement: Notes on Comparative and Development Administration." *Public Administration Review*, 36, 6 (November/December 1976), 648-654.

Response to critiques in items 17, 29, and 502. Notes that the Comparative Administration Group and comparative administration movement have been attacked but no coherent alternatives put forward. Defends CAG record and own theoretical work. Concludes with the observation that the globalization of problems will lead to a resurgence of comparative administration, albeit redefined, as the "master field" in which American public administration will be a subfield.

25. Robson, W. A. "The Study of Public Administration Then and Now." *Political Studies*, 23, 3 (June/September 1975), 193-201.

Discusses the changes that have taken place in the approach to teaching public administration in Britain in the last thirty five years. Draws contrasts with the United States, emphasizing the continuing institutional rather than behavioral emphasis of the British.

26. Savage, Peter. "Comparative Administration:
     An Assertion of Themes." *Comparative Poli-*
     tical Studies, 1, 2 (July 1968), 171-174.

     Introduction to an issue of *Comparative*
     Political Studies devoted entirely to compara-
     tive administration. Argues that given the
     fragmentary nature of the field there is a
     need to move beyond a "display of individual
     scholarly ingenuity" to "systematic explana-
     tion." This will be difficult, however,
     because of a lack of consensus on the terrain
     of comparative administration, differences
     over methodology, the practitioner vs. scholar
     debate, and the normative or ethical substance
     of the field.

27. Savage, Peter. "Optimism and Pessimism in
     Comparative Administration." *Public Ad-*
     ministration Review, 36, 4 (July/August
     1976), 415-423.

     General overview of the rise and decline of
     the comparative public administration movement
     in the United States. Notes that comparative
     public administration never developed a para-
     digm of its own, although Riggs's structural-
     functionalism came close. Still some successes
     of the movement are apparent: its concerns
     have been drawn into the mainstream of public
     administration; it has kept comparative poli-
     tics honest by stressing the importance of
     bureaucracy; and its focus on developing
     countries highlights values alternative to
     economy and efficiency.

28   Schaffer, Bernard B. "Comparisons, Administra-
     tion and Development." *Political Studies*,
     19, 3 (September 1971), 327-337.

     Reviews contributions of the Comparative
     Administration Group on the eve of its dis-
     solution. Notes its identification with
     development administration, ecological per-
     spectives, and Fred Riggs.

29. Sigelman, Lee. "In Search of Comparative
     Administration." *Public Administration
     Review*, 36, 6 (November/December 1976), 621-
     625.

     Assessment of the status of theory and
     research in comparative public administration.
     Provides content analysis of the *Journal of
     Comparative Administration* from 1969 through
     1974, and finds no common core of research
     issues, with no cumulation of knowledge.
     Argues against new conceptualizations and for
     new data gathering.

30. Smith, Gordan. "A Model of the Bureaucratic
     Culture." *Political Studies*, 22, 1 (1974),
     31-43.

     Posits, for comparative purposes, a general
     model of bureaucracy and politics that con-
     sists in two main dimensions: (1) the dis-
     tinctiveness of bureaucratic elites vis-a-vis
     the rest of society; and (2) the level of
     political involvement of these elites. Pro-
     duces a typology based on these dimensions,
     and illustrates with analysis of Austria.

31. Thomas, Rosamund. *The British Philosophy of
     Administration*. London: Longman, 1978.

     Compares underlying ideas of British public
     administration with those of America. Includes
     treatment of politics-administration dichoto-
     my, *Posdcorb* and ethics. Focuses on thought
     of six "contributors" to British philosophy
     of administration: Richard Haldane, Graham
     Wallas, William Beveridge, Josiah Stamp,
     Lyndall Urwick, and Oliver Sheldon.

32. Vidmer, Richard D. "Administrative Science
     in the U.S.S.R.: Doctrinal Constraints on
     "Inquiry." *Administration and Society*, 12,
     1 (May 1980), 69-92.

     The dominant paradigm in Soviet administra-

tive studies has five major elements: (1) preoccupation with organizational rationality;
(2) confusion of normative and empirical
tasks; (3) unitary notion of goals; (4)
stress on optimality as sole criterion of
evaluation; (5) domination of cybernetic-
systems terminology. This paradigm is rooted
in the Leninist tradition of organizational
leadership and Marx's scientific optimism.

33. Waldo, Dwight. "Comparative and Development
     Administration: Retrospect and Prospect."
     Public Administration Review, 36, 6 (Novem-
     ber/December 1976)

     Introduces comparative administration
     symposium (items 17, 24, 29 and 502), which
     grew out of a panel at the 1975 Annual Meet-
     ing of the American Political Science Associa-
     tion. Notes need for continued attention to
     comparative issues in the midst of a national
     turn inward in the late 1960's and early
     1970's.

34. Waldo, Dwight. "Public Administration and
     Change: Terra Paene Incognita." *Journal of
     Comparative Administration*, 1, 1 (May 1969),
     94-113.

     Before comparative public administration
     can contribute to change and development
     abroad, American public administration must
     learn to cope with turbulence and change at
     home. Public administration needs to articu-
     late a stronger theory and philosophy to
     define its identity.

CHAPTER 3

ADMINISTRATIVE HISTORY

The subject of this chapter is the History of Public Administration. All of the references in this chapter deal with the structures, roles or processes of bureaucracy in earlier times. Thus, unlike Chapter 2, the works cited here focus on the history of actual administrative systems, rather than on the history of ideas about administrative systems.

35. Barker, Ernest. *The Development of Public Services in Western Europe 1600-1930.* London: Oxford University Press, 1944.

    Historical analysis of the rise of bureaucracy in modern Europe. Focuses on France, Britain, and Prussia. Truly comparative, with treatments of conscription, taxation, social services, and education, as well as administration per se.

36. Beaglehole, T. H. "From Rulers to Servants: The I.C.S. and the British Demission of Power in India." *Journal of Developing Areas,* 11, 2 (April 1977), 237-256.

    Discusses the metamorphosis of the Indian Civil Service after the First World War. Focuses on the evolution of service and recruitment patterns in the interwar years. Describes tensions over "Indianization" and the Britsh belief that certain vital areas of administration would not be transferred to Indian hands without an extended period of tutelage.

37. Bendix, Reinhard. *Kings or People: Power and the Mandate to Rule.* Berkeley: University of California Press, 1973.

General study of the evolution of political authority and the idea of popular sovereignity. Uses a Weberian framework, and places a heavy emphasis on the role of bureaucratic (and patrimonial) officialdom in the process of historical transformation. Includes detailed analyses of Britain, France, Germany (Prussia), the Soviet Union and Japan.

38. Braibanti, Ralph, ed. *Asian Bureaucratic Systems Emergent from the British Imperial Tradition.* Durham: Duke University Press, 1966.

Eleven articles by leading students of Asian history and administration. Includes pieces on the British imperial heritage, bureaucratic change in India, civil service recruitment in India, the Pakistani civil service, and administration in Burma, Ceylon, Malaya and Nepal.

39. Burke, Fred G. "Public Administration in Africa: The Legacy of Inherited Colonial Institutions." *Journal of Comparative Administration*, 1, 3 (November 1969), 345-378.

Contrary to conventional wisdom, African administration is not especially influenced by traditional culture. The main constraint on administration for development is the legacy of colonial institutions. These were-- and are--maintenance and stability oriented. These institutions are powerfully reinforced by an inherited colonial "ecology" as well. Only the formulation of a new ideology can overcome this legacy.

40. Collins, Robert. "The Sudan Political
     Service: A Portrait of the Imperialists."
     African Affairs, 71, 284 (July 1972),
     293-303.

     Historical analysis of the Sudan Political
     Service, the elite group of British African
     colonial administrators. Covers period from
     inception in 1901 to disbanding in 1956.
     Focuses on the backgrounds and character of
     the men who comprised the Service. Argues
     that they were successful in welding together
     a state from the disparate parts and ethnic
     groups of the Sudan.

41. Creet, H. G. "The Beginnings of Bureaucracy
     in China." *Journal of Asian Studies*, 23, 2
     (February 1964), 155-184.

     Describes origin of bureaucracy in early
     China, circa third century B.C. Argues that
     bureaucracy is a contribution to world cul-
     ture like paper and gunpowder. Reviews early
     Chinese administrative theories and philoso-
     phies, which emphasized impartiality and
     impersonality.

42. de Vere, Allen J. "The Malayan Civil Service,
     1874-1941: Colonial Bureaucracy/Malayan
     Elite." *Comparative Studies in Society and
     History*, 12, 2 (April 1970), 149-178.

     Traces the development of the British
     colonial bureaucracy in the Malay states, with
     an emphasis on the growth and impact of the
     Malayan Civil Service (MCS). The MCS played
     a critical role in shaping Malay history in
     the 1920's and 1930's. Notes the growth in
     size of the MCS, the emergence of a distinc-
     tive esprit de corps, and the efforts to main-
     tain a certain independence from Whitehall.
     Includes tables of statistics.

43.   Dowdy, Edwin. *Japanese Bureaucracy: Its
      Development and Modernization*. Melbourne:
      Cheshire, 1972.

      Seeks to elucidate the elements in Japanese
      bureaucracy that have contributed to modern-
      ization. Account is primarily historical,
      with some sociological analysis. Modernizing
      impulses grew out of the social and cultural
      fabric of Japan, and were not mainly the
      result of foreign imprinting.

44.   Frank, Elke. "The Role of Bureaucracy in
      Transition." *Journal of Politics*, 28, 4
      (November, 1966), 724-753.

      Treats the issue of the role of bureaucracy
      in major regime transitions. Examines two
      cases in detail: the changeover from Imperial
      Germany to the Weimar Republic and the trans-
      formation of the Weimar Republic to the Third
      Reich. Concentrates on German Foreign Office.
      Includes some data on bureaucrats' party
      affiliations. Finds great stability in
      personnel and organization, although attempts
      at change were made.

45.   Gillis, J. R. *The Prussian Bureaucracy in
      Crisis, 1840-1860: Origins of an Adminis-
      trative Ethos*. Stanford, Stanford Univer-
      sity Press, 1971.

      Focuses narrowly on the operation of the
      Prussian bureaucracy during the reign of
      Frederick William IV. These were critical
      and formative years for the Prussian civil
      service, with a new bureaucratic ethos being
      formed that was to last until the overthrow
      of the monarchy in 1918. In particular, the
      bureaucracy was forced to adapt to the massive
      social and political changes sweeping through
      mid-nineteenth century Europe. Increased
      social heterogeneity led to a decline of
      the sense of esprit de corps and mission, and
      to an erosion of public confidence.

46. Gladden, E. N. *A History of Public Administration* (2 volumes). London: Frank Cass, 1972.

    Comprehensive description of the evolution of public bureaucracy. Study begins with earliest recorded administrative structures (Sumeria, 4,000 B.C.) and moves through some sixty-odd centuries to conclude with a discussion of modern public administration. These volumes are atheoretical, but descriptively thorough, with balanced treatments of Indian, Chinese, and American proto-bureaucracies, as well as European institutions.

47. Heper, Metin. "Political Modernization as Reflected in Bureaucratic Change: The Turkish Bureaucracy and a 'Historical Bureaucratic Empire' Tradition." *International Journal of Middle Eastern Studies,* 7, 4 (October 1976), 507-521.

    During the centuries of Ottoman political development, a bureaucracy-dominant polity developed which was loath to share power with other elites. Not until the 1960's was there a discernible softening of bureaucratic attitudes. Presents findings of survey of thirty-six administrative elites which confirm values of administrative hegemony.

48. Hogan, Mary Jane. "The Administration of Early Medieval England, With Special Reference to Northumberland." *Public Administration* (Sydney), 38, 3 (September 1979), 291-305.

    Describes the English administrative system from 1066 through 1350. Argues that administrative departments grew out of the royal household, and that the relatively great power of kings, in contradistinction to modern rulers, resulted from the much narrower scope of their administrative concerns.

49.   Jacoby, Henry. *The Bureaucratization of the World.* Berkeley: University of California Press, 1973.

      Extended essay on the evolution of bureaucracy. Integrates historical, economic, political, and philosophical analysis. Examples drawn from Western experience in general, although particular attention is given to the Russian case. Expresses fears of bureaucracy-democracy conflict. Like Weber, sees the key to survival in the activation of a politically responsible citizenry.

50.   Kooperman, Leonard and Stephen Rosenberg. "The British Administrative Legacy in Kenya and Ghana." *International Review of Administrative Sciences,* 43, 3 (1977), 267-272.

      In both Kenya and Ghana, the British failure to develop administrative capacity in the colonies led to many post-independence problems, including a persistent strain of administrative authoritarianism. At the same time, Britain bequeathed a legacy of civil service neutrality and impartiality.

51.   Lofstrom, William. "From Colony to Republic: A Case Study in Bureaucratic Change." *Journal of Latin American Studies,* 5, 2 (November 1973), 177-197.

      Describes administrative reform in nineteenth century Boliva. Traces intellectual roots to Francisco Suarez, a seventeenth century Spanish neo-Thomist. The product of bureaucratic change was the destruction of the last vestiges of the Spanish patrimonial state.

52.   Manchester, Alan K. "The Growth of Bureaucracy in Brazil, 1808-1821." *Journal of Latin American Studies,* 4, 1 (May 1972), 77-83.

Describes evolution of Brazilian bureaucracy
following arrival of John, Prince Regent of
Portugal, in Brazil in 1807. The creation of
an administrative apparatus in Brazil on the
Portuguese model created a centralized
national bureaucracy which looked to Rio de
Janeiro for authority.

53. Marx, Fritz Morstein. "The Higher Civil Serv-
ice as an Action Group in Western Political
Development." *Bureaucracy and Political
Development* (item 501).

The bureaucracy was a major contributor to
the political development of Western Europe,
increasing the viability of constitutional
government. An important historical change,
however, was the reorientation of the bureaucracy away from the concerns of government as
a whole to functional divisiveness. Describes
roles and action patterns of Western administrators, analyzing circumstances shaping
status quo versus reform orientations.

54. Misra, B. B. *The Bureaucracy in India: An
Historical Analysis of Development up to
1947.* Delhi: Oxford University Press, 1977.

Historically focused treatment of Indian
bureaucracy in the colonial period. Notes
disjuncture between modern values of bureaucracy and traditional values of society; this
stemmed from the British attempt to use the
machinery of the state as a lever of change
from the top (within the framework of im-
perialism). Pressures for "democratization"
took dysfunctional turns, however, leading
to communal separation and the erosion of
Indian Civil Service integrity.

55. Okada, T. "The Unchanging Bureaucracy."
Japan Quarterly, 12, 2 (April/June 1965),
168-176.

Historical examination of Japanese bureau-

cratization, from Meiji Restoration to present.
Aim is to understand underlying forces so as
to be able to undertake reform. The chief
problem with Japanese bureaucracy has been a
lack of popular control. Japanese political
parties remain subordinated to the bureaucracy.
There needs to be an effort made to restrict
political participation by bureaucrats.

56. Parris, Henry. *Constitutional Bureaucracy.*
London: George Allen and Unwin, 1969.

Historical analysis of the evolution of
British central government since the 1700's.
Constitutional bureaucracy is seen as equivalent to constitutional monarchy: beyond politics. Discusses the decline of patronage,
relationships between ministers and civil
servants, the characteristics of administrators, and some theoretical issues bearing on
the role of bureaucracy in government. Concludes with a critical analysis of reform
efforts.

57. Parris, Henry. "The Origins of the Permanent
Civil Service, 1780-1830." *Public Administration* (London), 46 (Summer 1968), 143-166.

Poses the question, "When did the British
Civil Service, qua service, start?" Argues
that it is inappropriate to date it prior
to 1780, since the eighteenth century administrative structure was not truly bureaucratic. Reviews reasons why no spoils system
gained root, and how administrators developed
professional autonomy. Concludes with an
examination of the origins of the permanent
secretaries, and a case study of their development in the Treasury.

58. Pinter, Walter M. "The Russian Higher Civil
Service on the Eve of the Great Reform."
Journal of Social History (Spring 1975),
55-68.

Examines the social background, training and career experience of leading Russian officials on the eve of the post-Crimean War reforms. Provides tables of data on fathers' status, serf ownership, and education. Concludes that the higher civil service in Russia at this time was undergoing class transformation through expansion of higher education.

59. Pinter, Walter M. "The Social Characteristics of the Early Nineteenth Century Russian Bureaucracy." *Slavic Review*, 29, 3 (1970), 429-443.

Descriptive statistical discussion of nineteenth century Russian officialdom. Based on records of 2,952 officials serving from 1846-1855, and 1,923 officials serving from 1798-1824. Provides data on nature of first employment, family serfholding, education, age, rank and social origins.

60. Pradhan, Prachanda. "The Nepalese Bureaucracy." *Philippine Journal of Public Administration*, 17, 2 (April 1973), 178-196.

Historical overview of Nepalese bureaucracy from 18th century to present. Notes difficulties adjusting to modernizing function since 1951 revolution.

61. Rigby, T.H. "The Birth of Soviet Bureaucracy." *Politics* (Australia), 3, 2 (November 1972), 121-135.

Discusses Soviet bureaucracy in historical perspective. Argues that Lenin's pragmatic practices were inconsistent with the revolutionary ideology he espoused. The *chinovnik* straitjacket was replaced by the *apparatchik* straitjacket, which was structurally similar and equally repressive.

62. Rosenberg, Hans. *Bureaucracy, Aristocracy and Autocracy: The Prussian Experience,*

1660-1815. Cambridge: Harvard University Press, 1958.

Classic study of the rise and institutionalization of the Prussian bureaucracy in the seventeenth and eighteenth centuries. Emphasizes the historical interaction of administrative officials with political elites and the socio-economic conditions that encouraged the development of bureaucratic hegemony.

63. Shinder, Joel. "Early Ottoman Administration in the Wilderness: Some Limits on Comparison." *International Journal of Middle Eastern Studies,* 9, 4 (November 1978), 497-517.

Reviews major interpretations of Ottoman institutional history. Argues against idea that there was a disruptive tension between the ideals of Islam and the practical needs of the state. Presents detailed analysis of the rise and functioning of the administrative class in the Ottoman empire.

64. Silberman, Bernard S. *Ministers of Modernization.* Tucson: University of Arizona Press, 1964.

Focuses on the emergence and development of the Japanese bureaucracy in the immediate post-Meiji restoration period. Analyzes the social backgrounds of the men who rose to positions of high bureaucratic power between 1868 and 1873. Finds that the post-1868 elite was drawn from the pre-1868 elite strata, although there is evidence of social mobility in the elevation of lower samurai to elite positions. Individual mobility was a product of Western education and inclination to engage in non-traditional political activity. The success of this group at modernization reflected in part strong national-local ties.

65. White, Leonard, Charles Bland, Walter Sharp
     and Fritz Morstein Marx. *Civil Service
     Abroad.* New York: McGraw-Hill, 1935.

     Four separate monographs on public personnel
     administration in Britain, Canada, France and
     Germany prepared by White, Bland, Sharp and
     Marx respectively for the Commission of In-
     quiry on Public Service Personnel, an advisory
     group formed to make recommendations to the
     Roosevelt Administration. Selections are
     historical and single-country focused.

66. Wright, Maurice. *Treasury Control of the Civil
     Service,* 1854-1874. Oxford: Clarendon Press,
     1969.

     Major historical analysis of the role of the
     Treasury in the nineteenth century as a con-
     troller of central government departmental
     spending. Begins with the issuance of the
     Northcote-Trevelyan report in 1854 and con-
     cludes with the Playfair Commission recom-
     mendations of 1874. Book is divided into four
     parts: (1) organizational description; (2)
     control of establishments; (3) control of con-
     ditions of service; and (4) concluding analy-
     ses. Includes detailed appendices with
     statistical data.

CHAPTER 4

BUREAUCRACY AND POLITICS

The complex relationships between bureaucrats and politicians are a major source of strain in all political systems, developing or developed, democratic or nondemocratic. As Max Weber recognized long ago, the unparalleled growth of bureaucracy in the modern age has both augmented and diminished the effective authority of political leaders. How political systems confront the challenge of bureaucracy has a marked effect on their character, performance and stability. This chapter provides references to works that seek to analyze this problem. Some are concerned mainly with mechanism of political control over bureaucracies (political parties, legislatures, and so forth) while others focus on the political role of bureaucrats themselves.

67. Adamolekum, Ladipo. "Accountability and Control Measures in Public Bureaucracies: A Comparative Analysis of Anglophone and Francophone Africa." *International Review of Administrative Sciences*, 40, 4 (1974), 307-321.

After examining the colonial heritage of Subsaharan Africa, analyzes four states-- Guinea, Tanzania, Nigeria and Senegal--in detail. The former are termed radical, and have adopted control mechanisms that rely on politicization of the civil service. The latter are termed conservative; these rely on more traditional mechanisms inherited from colonial powers. Nonetheless, there are continuities within the Anglophone and Francophone traditions.

68. Adamolekun, Ladipo. "Bureaucrats and the
     Senegalese Political Process." *Journal of
     Modern African Studies,* 9, 4 (October 1971),
     543-559.

     General study of the role of civil servants
     in Senegalese politics. Treats period from
     1957 to 1970. Finds intense bureaucratic
     participation. One reason for this is the
     country's French heritage, with its stress on
     career tenure. This involvement has had both
     positive and negative effects.

69. Alderman, R.K. and J.A. Cross. "Ministerial
     Reshuffles and the Civil Service." *British
     Journal of Political Science,* 9, 1 (January
     1979), 41-65.

     Assesses the impact of individual ministers'
     styles, tactics, ambition, and personality on
     their departments, and the effects of changes
     in ministerial leadership on departmental work-
     load and morale. Effort to redress typical
     academic concentration on the policy aspects
     of ministerial transitions. Concludes that
     ministerial-civil servant relations are
     structured by far more than policy considera-
     tions.

70. Allen, Douglas. "Ministers and their Manda-
     rins." *Government and Opposition,* 12, 2
     (Summer 1977), 135-149.

     The head of the British Home Civil Service
     reflects on the relationships between high-
     level administrators and ministers; from a
     speech to the London School of Economics.
     Outlines the proper role of the minister and
     of the permanent secretary, and discusses the
     need for teamwork between them. It is proper
     to say neither that the Civil Service runs the
     government nor that all government decisions
     are taken for reasons of short-term political
     advantage.

71. Anton, Thomas J. *Administered Politics: Elite
     Political Culture in Sweden.* Boston: Marti-
     nus Nijhoff Publishing, 1980.

     General study of administrative policy-making
     in Sweden. Seeks to understand how reformist
     policies can be reconciled with the supposed
     conservatism of public bureaucrats. Based on
     lengthy interviews with 312 senior civil ser-
     vants and 44 members of the Swedish parliament.
     Finds that while Swedish administrators are,
     to a considerable extent, conservative and
     rule-abiding , they see themselves as "problem-
     solvers" or "soft activists." This reduces
     the conflict between bureaucratic conservatism
     and social reform.

72. Anton, Thomas J., Claes Linde and Anders
     Mellbourn. "Bureaucrats in Politics: A
     Profile of the Swedish Administrative Elite."
     Canadian Public Administration, 16, 4 (Winter
     1973), 627-651.

     Surveys attitudes of Swedish administrative
     elite. Data drawn from interviews with more
     than 300 top-level civil servants. Suggests
     that Swedish "art of compromise" reflects
     bureaucrats' high degree of self-satisfaction,
     independence, and political sophistication.

*   Ashford, Douglas. "Resources, Spending and
     Party Politics in British Local Government."
     Cited as item 555.

73. Azrael, Jermy. *Managerial Power and Soviet
     Politics.* Cambridge: Harvard University
     Press, 1966.

     Examines the political role of Soviet in-
     dustrial managers in partial test of the
     hypothesis that economic development produces
     managerial elites predisposed toward greater
     freedom and democracy. Organized historically,
     with analysis beginning with pre-Bolshevik

period. Concludes that there is little foundation for the "new class" hypothesis. Soviet
technocrats have consistently bowed to the
political dictates of the regime.

74. Bachrach, Samuel B. and J. Lawrence French.
"Role-Allocation Processes in Public Bureau-
cracies." *Administration and Society*, 12, 4
(February 1981), 399-426.

Tests twelve hypotheses regarding the conditions necessary for merit-based or politically
neutral recruitment and promotion systems.
Sample of forty-four bureaucracies in Belgian
cities. In general, finds support for Weberian
contention that role allocation processes
linked closely to power-dependence relations
within and between organizations.

* Barnes, Samuel H. "Decision-Making in Italian
Local Politics: The View of the Communal
Councilor." Cited as item 556.

75. Barnett, A. Doak. "Mechanisms for Party Control in the Government Bureaucracy in China."
Asian Survey, 6, 12 (December 1966), 659-674.

All government organizations in the People's
Republic of China operate under close party
scrutiny. Major devices for control include:
"shadow" agencies in the party, monopolization
of key posts by party members and the use of
party fractions (party caucuses within organizations). In addition to control over administration in a geographic sense, the party is
also integrated in each functional area of
government.

76. Barnett, A. Doak and Ezra Vogel. *Cadres,
Bureaucracy, and Political Power in China*.
New York: Columbia University Press, 1967.

Detailed account, presented as three case
studies, of politics and government in a

Chinese ministry, county, and commune. Most
information based on interviews in Hong Kong
with ex-cadres. Confirms crucial role of the
party, although stresses also the growth of
bureaucratic social stratification. Includes
organizational charts, leadership structures
graphic representations of party-state relations in extensive appendices.

77. Beck, Carl. "Bureaucracy and Political Develop-
    ment in Eastern Europe." Bureaucracy and
    Political Development. (item 501).

    Describes and analyzes the impact of bureau-
    cratization on the political systems of
    Eastern Europe. Argues that standard bureau-
    cratic analysis is not adequate for explain-
    ing political development here. The political
    systems of Eastern Europe have generally
    adapted to modernity without succumbing to
    excessive bureaucratization. Totalitarian sys-
    tems must be seen as systems. That is, they
    are subject to pressures from the external
    environment that create situations requiring
    adaptation and change.

78. Beck, Carl et al. Comparative Communist Poli-
    tical Leadership. New York: David McKay,
    1973.

    Collection of seven essays dealing with
    administrative and political elites in Eastern
    Europe, the Soviet Union and China. Intro-
    ductory article (by William Welsh) deals with
    theoretical and methodological issues.

79. Beneviste, Guy. Bureaucracy and National Plan-
    ning: A Sociological Case Study in Mexico.
    New York: Praeger, 1970.

    Planning is a political process, and within
    bureaucracies successful planners must build
    winning coalitions. This argument is illustra-
    ted in a case study of educational planning

in Mexico. Describes the chief actors--
Ministry of Education, state governments,
businessmen, church--and the historical background of the National Commission for Overall
Planning of Education. Concludes with the
observation that planners themselves did not--
and generally do not--understand themselves
the political roles they must play.

80.   Bhambri, Chandra P. *Bureaucracy and Politics
       in India*. Dehli: Vikas, 1971.

       Focuses on bureaucrat-politician interaction
       at top levels of Indian government. Starts
       from the assumption that strong political
       parties are necessary to control bureaucracy.
       Presents series of case studies of inter-
       actions between administrative and political
       elites. Concludes that India is in danger of
       succumbing to bureaucratic hegemony. Suggests
       restructuring the system and installing new
       controls on administration.

81.   Brown-John, C. Lloyd. "Party Politics and the
       Canadian Federal Public Service." *Public
       Administration* (London), 52 (Spring 1974),
       79-94.

       Reports on the impact of the 1967 Public Ser-
       vice Employment Act, which granted Canadian
       federal public servants the right to partici-
       pate actively in party politics. Examines
       applicants for leaves to stand as party candi-
       dates, and provides tabular analyses by
       ministries, type of election, territory, and
       party.

*   Caiden, Gerald. "Coping with Turbulence:
       Israel's Administrative Experience." Cited
       as item 343.

*   Camp, Roderic Al. "The Cabinet and the Tech-
       nico in Mexico and the United States."
       Cited as item 179.

82. Chai, Trong R. "Communist Party Control over
     the Bureaucracy: the Case of China." *Compara-*
     tive Politics, 11, 3 (April 1979), 359-370.

     Assesses the extent to which the Chinese
     Communist party exercised effective control
     over the bureaucracy by examining the turnover
     patterns of ministers and commission chairmen
     in 38 ministries from 1949-1969. Concludes
     that Mao's control was very weak on the eve of
     the cultural revolution (1965), rebounding only
     slightly thereafter. In general, the idea that
     formal Communist authorities are able to keep
     a close check on bureaucracy is overstated.
     It is important to examine the interactions
     between party factions and the bureaucracy
     instead.

83. Chevallier, Jacques. "L'intérêt Général dans
     l'Administration Française." *International*
     Review of Administrative Sciences, 41, 4
     (1975), 325-350.

     Explores the central idea of "general inter-
     est" in French administration, which is used
     to justify a wide range of bureaucratic actions.
     In particular, the notion of a "general inter-
     est" has helped strengthen hierarchy and per-
     petuate the existing social structure.

84. Cleaves, Peter S. *Bureaucratic Politics and*
     Administration in Chile. Berkeley: Univer-
     sity of California Press, 1974.

     Focuses on Chilean administrative politics
     during the Frei regime (1964-1970). Data
     drawn from 150 indepth interviews with
     Chilean elites. Rejects traditional compara-
     tive administration frameworks (ecological,
     class, development, etc), and uses a bureau-
     cratic politics/political economy approach.
     Emphasizes organizational strategies and
     tactics. Case material centers on housing
     programs.

85. Damgaard, Erik. "The Political Role of Non-
     political Bureaucrats in Denmark." *The
     Mandarins of Western Europe: The Political
     Role of Top Civil Servants* (item 91).

          Following an outline of the Danish adminis-
     trative system, argues that civil servants
     exercise an important role in political
     decision-making. This is in large part due
     to the failure of political elites to take
     action to counter the strength of bureaucrats.
     Unless politicians do act, bureaucratic in-
     volvement will increase in the future.

86. Dang Nghiem. *Viet-Nam: Politics and Public
     Administration*. Honolulu: East-West Center
     Press, 1966.

          Applies ecological model to administration in
     Vietnam. Describes basic philosophy of Viet-
     namese public administration and outlines
     structures of government (in the South).
     Separate chapters devoted to personnel, finan-
     cial administration, decision-making, and
     communication.

87. de Lamothe, A. Dutheillet. "Ministerial
     Cabinets in France." *Public Administration*
     (London), 43 (Winter 1965), 365-381.

          Member of the Conseil d'Etat outlines the
     structure and functions of the "cabinet du
     ministre," and relates it to the general role
     of the Grands Corps. Ministerial cabinets,
     consisting of the personal aides of each
     minister, are "bridges which join administra-
     tion and politics."

88. Denton, Charles F. "Bureaucracy in an Immobil-
     ist Society: The Case of Costa Rica."
     Administrative Science Quarterly, 14, 3
     (September 1969), 418-425.

Overview of Costa Rican administration using
a Riggsian ecological model. Data drawn from
survey of bureaucrats in two public agencies
are presented. Argues for three major propositions: (1) strong political parties do not
necessarily lead to institutional development; (2) immobilist politics lead to immobilist administration; and (3) the politics/
administration dichotomy is no more relevant
for Costa Rica than for economically developed
societies.

89.   Dittmer, Lowell.   "Revolution and Reconstruc-
      tion in Contemporary Chinese Bureaucracy."
      Journal of Comparative Administration, 5, 4
      (February 1974), 443-486.

      Examines the Maoist critique of bureaucracy
      and the effect of the Cultural Revolution on
      the Chinese administrative apparatus. Attempts
      to decentralize authority and to democratize
      recruitment were partially successful, but a
      tension remains with the corresponding effort
      to make the system responsive to central
      leadership. Suggests that the situation is
      too fluid to allow firm predictions about
      institutionalization of Maoist reform.

90.   Divine, Donna R.   "The Modernization of the
      Israeli Administration." *International
      Journal of Middle Eastern Studies*, 5, 3
      (June 1974), 295-313.

      There is a consensus among social scientists
      that Israel may be considered a developed
      nation in virtually all things save those
      administrative. Israeli public administra-
      tion is held to be "stunted" because of
      political interference. Tests this assumption
      by studying the relative influence of party
      affiliation and education/experience on civil
      service advancement. Finds that party politi-
      cal activity is relatively unrelated to
      advancement.

91.   Dogan, Mattei, ed. *The Mandarins of Western
       Europe: The Political Role of Top Civil
       Servants*. New York: Sage Publications,
       1975.

       Fourteen essays on higher civil servants in
       Western Europe. Includes items 85, 92, 119,
       122, 133, 430.

92.   Dogan, Mattei. "The Political Power of the
       Western Mandarins: Introduction." *The
       Mandarins of Western Europe: The Political
       Role of Top Civil Servants*. (item 91).

       Introduces edited volume on political roles
       of higher civil servants in Western Europe.
       Discusses the expanding power of state
       bureaucracies and the corollary decline of
       parliaments. Categorizes types of mandarins
       based on degrees of political power and
       partisanship. Concludes that too much power
       has been "displaced" to civil servants.

93.   Encarnation, Dennis J. "The Indian Central
       Bureaucracy: Responsive to Whom?" *Asian
       Survey*, 19, 11 (November 1979), 1126-1145.

       Analyzes Indian bureaucracy in terms of its
       external and internal "political economics."
       Suggests that picture of bureaucracy as un-
       responsive is inaccurate. Bureaucracy is
       responsive--but chiefly to powerful economic
       claimants.

*   Fried, Robert. *The Italian Prefects: A
       Study in Administrative Politics*. Cited as
       item 565.

*   Gibbons, David S. and Haji Ahmad Zakaria.
       "Politics and Selection for the Higher
       Civil Service in New States: The Malaysian
       Experience." Cited as item 212.

94. Gordon, Michael R. "Civil Servants, Politi-
     cians and Parties: Shortcomings in the
     British Policy Process." Comparative
     Politics, 4, 1 (October 1971), 29-58.

     For many years, the British Civil Service
     was all but impenetrable to the outside
     observer. The precise role of the adminis-
     trator in the policy process was unknown.
     The Fulton Report provided a great deal of
     new information, as have other accounts in
     the 1960's. It is now clear that the twin
     doctrines of ministerial responsibility and
     civil service neutrality do not work as
     smoothly as theory predicts, leading to
     difficulties in party government.

95. Grindle, Merilee S. "Power, Expertise and
     the 'Technico': Suggestions From a Mexican
     Case Study." Journal of Politics, 39, 2
     (May 1977), 399-426.

     Dissatisfaction with traditional bureau-
     crats plus a need for creativity and dyna-
     mism in administration have led to increased
     interest in the "technico," or the "new man
     of knowledge" in Latin American governments.
     Suggests that technicos combine expertise
     and political power. Data drawn from inter-
     views with high and middle level officials
     of Conasupo, a Mexican agency that regulates
     the market for basic commodities. Concludes
     that more realistic models for reform of
     Latin bureaucracies are needed--models that
     do not insist on dichotomizing technicos and
     politicos.

*   Grindle, Merilee S. Bureaucrats, Politicians,
     and Peasants in Mexico: A Case Study in
     Public Policy. Cited as item 489.

96. Groves, Roderick T. "The Colombian National
     Front and Administrative Reform." Adminis-
     tration and Society, 6, 3 (November 1974),

316-336.

Most of the goals of the administrative
reform effort begun in Colombia in 1953 have
been achieved, most notably in the areas of
reorganization and budgeting. The success of
the process is due to the National Front
political system which provided political
stability and political leadership. The
problem, though, is that there is little
evidence that administrative reform itself
has contributed to social change or national
development.

97. Harris, Richard L. "The Effects of Political
    Change on the Role Sets of the Senior
    Bureaucrats in Ghana and Nigeria." *Adminis-
    trative Science Quarterly*, 13, 3 (December
    1968), 386-401.

    As in developed political systems, elite
    administrators in the developing world have
    multifunctional roles. Changes in the goals
    or structure of the political system will
    effect changes in those roles. Ghana and
    Nigeria are used to illustrate this point.
    Three major propositions are set forth: (1)
    similarity of background of political and
    bureaucratic elites will determine whether
    administrative roles are expanded or con-
    tracted; (2) administrative roles will be
    expanded after a regime change if bureaucratic
    skills are necessary to accomplish new goals;
    (3) when new political leaders see their own
    roles expansively, they will restrict the
    roles of senior bureaucrats; the converse is
    also true.

98. Harris, Richard L. "The Role of the Civil
    Servant in West Africa." *Public Adminis-
    tration Review*, 24, 4 (December 1965), 308-
    313.

    The role of the civil servant in Africa
    departs from Western neutrality and is heavily
    affected by the political environment. While

the responsibilities of administrators have
increased, their abilities to discharge them
effectively have been constrained by a lack
of political consensus, low political morality,
political favoritism and one-party rule.

99. Harris, Richard L. and Robert N. Kearney.
     "A Comparative Analysis of the Administra-
     tive Systems of Canada and Ceylon."
     Administrative Science Quarterly, 8, 3
     (December 1963), 339-360.

     Uses an ecological or environmental approach
     in an effort to compare Canadian and Ceylonese
     administration. Attempts to identify the
     cultural variables influencing public
     administration in an industrially well-
     developed Western state and a developing
     nation. Major influences discussed are (1)
     geographic and economic; (2) social environ-
     ment; and (3) political environment.

100. Hawker, Geoffrey. "The Bureaucracy Under the
     Whitlam Government." *Politics* (Australia),
     10, 1 (May 1975), 15-23.

     Describes changes that Labour Government
     has made in organizational deployment and
     management of the public services. Argues
     that the reforms are marginal to date, but
     will provide a broad base for agreement among
     parties.

101. Heper, Metin. "The Recalcitrance of the
     Turkish Public Bureaucracy to Bourgeois
     Politics." *Middle Eastern Journal*, 30, 4
     (Autumn 1976), 485-500.

     Contrasts historical development of Turkish
     bureaucracy with Western European model in
     terms of relationship to rising bourgeoisie.
     The Turkish pattern was one of "induced"
     rather than "organic" change. Analyzes the
     relationship between the two foremost elite

groups in Turkish Society--the bureaucracy
and entrepreneurial groups. Due to the
wealth and status of business groups, the
Turkish bureaucracy feels a "status discrepan-
cy" which leads to radical and pathological
behavior.

102. Heper, Metin, Chong Lim Kim and Seong-Tong
     Pai. "The Role of Bureaucracy and Regime
     Types." *Administration and Society*, 12, 2
     (August 1980), 137-157.

     Tests the proposition: Do political roles
     of bureaucracies vary with regime type?
     Analyzes data based on interviews with 232
     Turkish and 225 Korean civil servants. Finds
     no support in favor of regime type predicting
     roles.

*   Higley, John, Karl Erik Brofoss, and Knut
     Groholt. "Top Civil Servants and the
     National Budget in Norway." Cited as item
     430.

103. Hopkins, Raymond F. *Political Roles in a New
     State*. New Haven and London: Yale Univer-
     sity Press, 1971.

     Empirical study of elite role orientation
     in Tanzania. Three role sets--administrative,
     legislative and presidential--and their inter-
     actions described in detail. Interviews con-
     ducted with 58 M.P.'s and 51 administrators.
     Argues that a culture of "closed politics,
     which seeks to contain political dissent,"
     is emerging in Tanzania.

104. Jahan, Rounaq. "Ten Years of Ayub Khan and
     the Problem of National Integration."
     Journal of Comparative Administration, 2, 3
     (November 1970), 277-298.

     Seeks to test the validity of the proposi-
     tion which holds that military regimes are

more effective than civilian regimes in bringing about national integration. Analyzes case
of Pakistan. Finds that the regime failed to
reflect national diversity in elite recruitment and failed to develop counterbalancing
participatory mechanisms at local levels. A
high rate of economic growth was not accompanied by an equitable system of distribution.

105. Kernaghan, Kenneth. "Politics, Policy and
     Public Servants: Political Neutrality
     Revisited." *Canadian Public Administration*,
     19, 3 (Fall 1976), 432-456.

     The traditional model of civil service neu-
     trality is inadequate to describe the politi-
     cal involvement of public servants. Detailed
     examination of Canadian case presented. Pub-
     lic servants in Canada are actively involved
     in policy development and execution.

106. Korbonski, Andrezej. "Bureaucracy and
     Interest Groups in Communist Societies:
     The Case of Czechoslovakia." *Studies in
     Comparative Communism*, 4, 1 (January 1971),
     57-79.

     Describes relationship between bureaucracy
     and interest groups through role of each in
     the debate surroudning the Czechoslovak
     economic reforms of 1964-1967. Argues that
     gradual decline in the role of ideology has
     led to widespread bureaucratization and that
     the emergence of a degree of pluralism has
     produced broader roles and greater importance
     for interest groups.

107. Krauss, Wilma R. "Toward a Theory of Politi-
     cal Participation of Public Bureaucrats."
     Administrative Science Quarterly, 16, 2
     (June 1971), 180-191.

     Examines participation in electoral politics
     of Hawaiian and Filipino bureaucrats. Data
     drawn from survey of 52 mid-level Filipino

bureaucrats and 57 Hawaiian mid-level administrators. Finds that in merit system, participation varies with hierarchical structure,
length of service and income. In patronage
system, participation varies with party
preference. Concludes with a generalized
theoretical model of political participation
of bureaucrats.

108. Kringen, John A. "An Exploration of the 'Red-
Expert' Issue in China Through Content
Analysis." *Asian Survey*, 15, 8 (August
1975), 693-707.

The 'red-expert' distinction has largely
been treated in ideal-typical, abstract
terms. Data from 81 Chinese documents are
content-analyzed to see how the words actually
are used. Finds great multi-dimensionality
in usage. Suggests greater focus on organizational factors and other lines of conflict
rather than red vs. expert split to explain
Chinese politics.

109. Lee, Hahn-Been. *Korea: Time, Change, and
Administration*. Honolulu: East-West Center
Press, 1963.

Examines the relationship between political-
administrative environment and administrative
development during post-liberation period.
Uses time-orientation approach as framework
of analysis. Includes discussion of ideological and institutional changes in governmental environment through 1963. Argues that
political leadership must be innovative to
accelerate modernization.

110. Levine, William. "Statesmen and Civil Ser-
vants in African Development." *Studies in
Comparative International Development*, 2, 1
(Spring 1976), 63-87.

Discusses the relationship between civil

servants and statesmen engaged in the
development process. Suggests analytical
framework consisting of resource and execution
dimensions, as well as dimension pertaining to
the legitimation of authority.

111. Maniruzzaman, Talukder. "Administrative Reforms and Politics Within the Bureaucracy
in Bangladesh." *Journal of Commonwealth
Political Studies*, 17, 1 (March 1979), 47-
59.

Bangladesh's bureaucracy is not only relatively small, but it is riddled with conflict.
Some cleavages are ideological, others are
factional, others still are sectarian. Reviews attempt to reform and reorganize the
civil service under various regimes.

112. Marican, Y.M. "Bureaucratic Power in India
and Japan." *Philippine Journal of Public
Administration*, 16, 2 (April 1972), 204-
220.

Comparative study of "politics and administration" in India and Japan. Finds greater
bureaucratic autonomy and influence in Japan.
Indian bureaucrats are far more subordinate
to politicians.

113. Marković, R. "Le Rôle du Droit dans le
Travail de l'Administration Publique--
Avec un Aperçu Spécial sur la Yougoslavie
et l'U.R.S.S." *International Review of
Administrative Sciences*, 41, 2 (1975), 159-
180.

Analyzes five sets of devices in socialist
countries, particularly Yugoslavia and the
Soviet Union, to make administrative behavior
conform to the law. These include: (1)
political controls; (2) administrative controls; (3) judicial controls; (4) controls by
the procureur, or controller general; and (5)
controls by constitutional courts in

Yugoslavia.

114. Mayntz, Renate and Fritz W. Scharpf. *Policy-Making in the German Federal Republic.* Amsterdam: Elsevier, 1975.

Focuses on the role of German bureaucracy in policy-making, with special attention to ways to improve its "problem-solving capabilities." Describes contemporary structure of the system, including personnel procedures. Outlines departmental organization and relationships of politicians and administrators. Includes some data on civil servant attitudes. Concludes with recommendations for structural reform.

115. Meijer, Hans. "Bureaucracy and Policy Formulation in Sweden." *Scandinavian Political Studies,* 4 (1969), 103-116.

Focuses on the role of special advisory commissions in Swedish administration. These are used frequently as a way to engender consensus on difficult issues. Although this decisional process is often painfully slow, it does mean smoother implementation once a policy is adopted, since all parties have been involved in planning. Includes data on character and composition of commissions.

116. Merikoski, V. "The Politicization of Public Administration." *International Review of Administrative Sciences,* 39, 3 (1973), 211-224.

Examines the influence of party politics on administration, drawing heavily on the Finnish experience, but with some reference to other Nordic states, as well as Britain and the United States. Argues in behalf of strict neutrality of all non-political civil servants.

117. Miller, Robert A. "The Party-State and Bureau-
cratic/Political Relations in Africa."
Comparative Political Studies, 8, 3 (October
1975), 293-317.

Analyzes extent to which the distinction
between bureaucrat and politician has been
blurred in Tanzania, as one would predict
using a party-state model. Data base consists in social background characteristics
for 342 Ugandan and 356 Tanzanian elites.
Finds that, contrary to expectations, social
background differences less in Uganda, a non-
party-state.

118. Mills, G.E. "The Environment of Commonwealth
Caribbean Bureaucracies." *International
Review of Administrative Sciences,* 39, 1
(1973), 14-24.

Discusses range of Caribbean countries,
including the Bahamas, British Honduras,
Trinidad and Tobago and Guyana. Analyzes
ecological influences on administration, which
provide a basis for some commonalities among
these states, as well as sources of tension
and conflict peculiar to each such as race,
class, and education.

119. Moulin, Léo. "The Politicization of the
Administration in Belgium." *The Mandarins
of Western Europe: The Political Role of
Top Civil Servants* (item 91).

Public administration in Belgium is highly
politicized. Although this has always been
true, it is more apparent now since the
nineteenth century political consensus among
societal elites has given way to antagonism.
Administrative careers are shaped by language,
class, political leanings, religion, region,
and patron-client links. This has transformed political parties into "placement
offices" for higher civil servants.

120. Nelsen, Harvey W. "Military Bureaucracy in the Cultural Revolution." *Asian Survey,* 14, 4 (April 1974), 372-395.

 The cultural revolution failed either to reduce the overall size of the bureaucracy or to increase its responsiveness to direction from above. Any reduction in civilian numbers was compensated by increased involvement of the Army in governmental functions. A study of leadership at provincial and local levels reveals that central control is extremely limited. Although the new elite now more often wears military uniforms than blue suits, a self-interested "revisionist" elite is still in charge.

121. Nowak, Thomas C. "The Philippines Before Martial Law: A Study in Politics and Administration." *American Political Science Review,* 71, 2 (June 1977), 522-539.

 Describes the development of patronage-based political-bureaucratic machines in the post-World War II to pre-martial law (1972) Philippines. Argues that these machines, rooted in local administration, generated expenditure patterns viewed as "wasteful" by businessmen and technocrats.

122. Passigli, Stefano. "The Ordinary and Special Bureaucracies in Italy." *The Mandarins of Western Europe: The Political Role of Top Civic Servants* (item 91).

 Contrasts operation of traditional ministries ("ordinary bureaucracies") in Italy with "special agencies," those primarily concerned with economic direction and regulation. The latter are far more important in producing governmental "outputs."

123. Pempel, T.J. "The Bureaucratization of Policymaking in Postwar Japan." *American Journal of Political Science,* 18, 4

(November 1974), 647-664.

Examines four indicators of bureaucratic
penetration of Japanese policy-making: independence of the Diet; Liberal-Democratic
Party-bureaucracy links; the bureaucracy's
use of "ordinance" (regulation) power; and
bureaucratic control of "independent" advisory
committees. All indicators point to a large
and growing role for the Japanese bureaucracy in policy-making.

124. Peters, Guy B. *The Politics of Bureaucracy:
    A Comparative Perspective.* New York: Long-
    man, 1978.

    General text-like overview of public
    administrative written from a comparative
    perspective. Includes chapters on growth of
    government, political culture, recruitment,
    politics and administration, and administra-
    tive accountability. Examples drawn mostly
    from Western Europe, though there is not a
    focus on any single country or area.

125. Poitras, Guy E. and Charles F. Denton.
    "Bureaucratic Performance: Case Studies
    from Mexico and Costa Rica." *Journal of
    Comparative Administration,* 3, 2 (August
    1971), 169-187.

    Develops hypotheses derived from Ferrel
    Heady's arguments about the relationships
    between regime type and bureaucratic behavior
    (see item 8). Costa Rica is considered
    "polyarchal-competitive," Mexico "dominant
    party, semi-competitive." After an analysis
    of three case studies, finds some support
    for Heady's contention. Bureaucratic per-
    formance, as perceived by bureaucrats, may
    be enhanced by political systems that restrain
    competitive tendencies.

126. Porter, John. *The Vertical Mosaic: An Analysis of Social Class and Power in Canada.* Toronto: University of Toronto Press, 1965.

Major empirical study of class and status in Canada. Although only one chapter (of 17) is devoted to the Canadian federal bureaucracy, contains useful background information on Canadian society.

127. Putnam, Robert D., Aberbach, Joel D. and Bert A. Rockman. *Bureaucrats and Politicians in Western Democracies.* Cambridge: Harvard University Press, 1981.

Asks, how are politicians and bureaucrats similar to and different from one another in Western Europe? Finds that they differ on several important dimensions, including education, family background, and orientations. Pulls together empirical work from the University of Michigan comparative elites project on the U.S., Britain, Germany, France and Netherlands. Develops a typology of bureacratic actors, with main criterion role in policy formulation. Finds that bureaucratic participation in policymaking is widespread and growing, and that tensions with politicians are inevitable.

128. Putnam, Robert D. "The Political Attitudes of Senior Civil Servants in Western Europe: A Preliminary Report." *British Journal of Political Science,* 3, 3 (July 1973), 257-290.

Presents partial results of major study (item 119) of political and administrative elites in Britain, France, West Germany, Sweden, Italy, the Netherlands, and the United States. Focus here is on Britain, Germany and Italy. Central purpose is to assess attitudes and orientation through in-depth interviews. Distinguishes between "classical" and "political" bureaucrats, and discusses variations of types across national systems.

129. Pyne, Peter. "The Bureaucracy in the Irish
     Republic: Its Political Role and the
     Factors Influencing it." *Political Studies*,
     22, 1 (March 1974), 15-30.

     General analysis of Irish bureaucracy. De-
     scribes its functions and the environment with-
     in which it operates. Concludes that the
     Irish public service has been quite successful,
     especially in comparison to the services of
     today's developing countries. It is neutral
     as well as politically responsive.

130. Rahman, A.T.R. "Administration and Its
     Political Environment in Bangladesh."
     Pacific Affairs, 47, 2 (Summer 1974), 171-
     191.

     Analyzes changing relationship between
     administration and its political environment
     in Bangladesh. Argues that the pattern of
     administrative dominance established during
     the British raj has begun to reverse itself.
     Political parties and interest groups are
     becoming stronger and more assertive. Con-
     cludes that there are conflicts, however,
     between democratic aspirations and partisan
     institution-building.

*   Rawin, Solomon John. "Social Values and the
     Managerial Structure." Cited below as item
     384.

131. Ronge, Volker. "The Politicization of
     Administration in Advanced Capitalist
     Societies." *Political Studies*, 22, 1
     (March 1974), 86-93.

     Routine administrative decision-making no
     longer can be legitimized by general diffuse
     support for government, which is becoming
     increasingly difficult to mobilize. Instead,
     specific support must be sought, which is
     leading to a greater politicization of
     administration.

132. Roos, Leslie L., Jr. and Noralou P. Roos.
     "Administrative Change in a Modernizing
     Society." *Administrative Science Quarterly,*
     15, 1 (March 1970), 69-78.

     Political competition leads to a decline of
     bureaucratic influence in politics. In Tur-
     key, at least, bureaucrats responded favorably
     to this change in position. Study based on
     survey data collected at two points--1956
     and 1965--to examine recruitment and job
     satisfaction over time. Concludes that by
     1965 a new focus on technical concerns had
     displaced the former political and social
     conflicts in the Turkish bureaucracy.

133. Ruffieux, Roland. "The Political Influence
     of Senior Civil Servants in Switzerland."
     *The Mandarins of Western Europe: The Politi-
     cal Role of Top Civil Servants* (item 91).

     The Swiss civil service is quite democratic
     in character, resembling neither the French
     nor Prussian types. Nevertheless, it has
     considerable political power, owing to the
     increased scope of governmental activities.

134. Scarman, Lord Justice. "Public Administra-
     tion and the Courts." *Public Administration*
     (London), 79 (Spring 1979), 1-6.

     Although British courts traditionally re-
     frained from interfering with executive acts,
     recently they have begun to expand their
     scope of competence. The lack of any written
     constitutional principles that might clarify
     relative executive and judicial responsibili-
     ties has created great uncertainty. Reviews
     recent case law.

*   Schmidt, Steffen W. "Bureaucrats as Modern-
     izing Brokers? Clientalism in Colombia."
     Cited below as item 624.

* Schumacher, Edward J. *Politics, Bureaucracy and Rural Development in Senegal.* Cited below as item 532.

135. Sigelman, Lee. "Do Modern Bureaucracies Dominate Underdeveloped Polities? A Test of the Imbalance Thesis." *American Political Science Review*, 66, 2 (June 1972), 525-528.

Examines proposition that administrative modernity promotes overparticipation by bureaucrats in governmental functions. Analyzes judgmental data on fifty-seven Latin American, African and Asian nations. Finds high <u>negative</u> correlation between administrative development and overparticipation. Suggests that this key premise of comparative administration needs to be reconsidered.

* Spencer, Chuku-Dinka R. "Politics, Public Administration and Agricultural Development: A Case Study of the Sierra Leone Industrial Plantation Development Program, 1964-67." Cited as item 539.

136. Subramaniam, V. "Politicized Administration in Africa and Elsewhere: A Socio-historical Analysis." *International Review of Administrative Sciences*, 43, 4 (1977), 297-308.

While African Commonwealth countries inherited many aspects of the British civil service, they failed to allow tradition of civil service neutrality to take root. It eroded in Africa faster than in Asia owing to shorter period of rule, compressed independence struggles, and need to mobilize masses quickly by parties.

137. Suleiman, Ezra. *Politics, Power and Bureaucracy in France.* Princeton: Princeton University Press, 1974.

Focuses on the role of higher administration
in French government. Describes background
and attitudes of administrative elite, and
their relationships with politicians, ministers, and interest groups. Based on extensive
in-depth interviews (interview schedule included in appendix). Concludes that while the
French civil service is unrepresentative of
French society, it is not wholly unresponsive.

138. Thomas, Ladd. "Bureaucratic Attitudes and
      Behavior as Obstacles to Political Integra-
      tion of Thai Muslims." *Southeast Asia*, 3,
      1 (1974), 545-568.

      The forces of history have separated the
      Thai Muslims from the rest of the Thai people.
      Efforts to integrate them have faltered in
      part because of negative bureaucratic atti-
      tudes. Data drawn from interviews with 108
      Thai bureaucrats. Statistics presented in
      tabular form.

139. Tice, Robert D. "Administrative Structure,
      Ethnicity, and Nation-Building in the Ivory
      Coast." *Journal of Modern African Studies*,
      12, 2 (June 1974), 211-230.

      The internal administrative "spatial struc-
      ture" of the Ivory Coast has deliberately been
      used by the government as a focal point of
      Ivoirian identification in an effort to foster
      national integration.

140. Tsoutsos, Athos. "Administration Publique
      et Politique." *International Review of
      Administrative Sciences*, 44, 4 (1978),
      323-332.

      After a general theoretical discussion of
      the politics-administration dichotomy and
      associated issues in Western democracies,
      comments on the Greek case.

141 Vogel, Ezra F. "From Revolutionary to Semi-
Bureaucrat: The Regularization of Cadres."
China Quarterly, 29 (January/March 1967),
36-60.

Describes the transformation of revolutionary cadres into administrators in postrevolutionary China. Notes the vastly different role expectations, and the shift in training required. Concludes with discussion of
problems of salary and career development.

142. Volti, Rudi. "Organizations and Expertise in
China." *Administration and Society*, 8, 4
(February 1977), 423-458.

The traditional dichotomy between "reds"
and "experts" made by analysts of Chinese
bureaucracy is inadequate. Both categories
have multiple dimensions. Moreover, organizational affiliation is important in defining
the role of the expert in China.

143. von der Mehden, Fred R. "The Military and
Development in Thailand." *Journal of
Comparative Administration*, 2, 2 (November
1970), 323-340.

Thailand made progress in economic and social
development under military rule. However,
this development took place in the context of
uneasy relations between military, civilian
bureaucracy and business sectors. Little
systematic planning or coordination was forthcoming.

144. Wright, Vincent. "Politics and Administration Under the French Fifth Republic."
Political Studies, 22, 1 (March 1974), 44-
65.

Examines the extent to which the French
Government has become a "Republique des
fonctionnaires" or a republic of administrators. Systematically evaluates the positions

of those who argue that the bureaucracy has become too powerful, and then moves to an analysis of the opposite position. Concludes that the situation is more tangled than either side would have it.

145. Ziller, Jacques. "Hauts Fonctionnaires et Politique en République Fédérale d'Allemagne." *International Review of Administrative Sciences*, 47, 1 (1981), 31-41.

Examines the relationship between senior civil servants and politics in West Germany. Notes growing problems with the practice of designating certain high officials as "political civil servants." Although their rights are largely protected, there are moves to develop institutions similar to French ministerial cabinets to allow such officials the opportunity to undertake temporary terms of office without jeopardizing their civil service status. Notes overall blurring of lines between politics and administration at this level, although in a different way than has occurred in France.

* Ziring, Lawrence and Robert LaPorte Jr. "The Pakistan Bureaucracy: Two Views." Cited below as item 553.

CHAPTER 5

PERSONNEL ADMINISTRATION

The subfield of personnel administration is
very broad. It is concerned with a wide variety
of problems and procedures that bear on the
recruitment, training, and management of public
employees, including the nature of the administrative structure within which the employees are
housed. This chapter reflects this breadth and
diversity. Among the major questions addressed
by the works cited herein are: Why are certain
people selected as employees? What sort of training is most useful? How should personnel offices
be organized? What difficulties are encountered
in establishing merit-based civil service systems
in developing countries? Also included in this
chapter are references to general works that describe the overall administrative structures of
different countries.

146. Abbas, M.B.A. "Public Administration Train-
      ing in Pakistan: A Critical Appraisal."
      *International Review of Administrative
      Sciences*, 36, 3 (1970), 256-270.

      Pakistan's British administrative heritage
      did not place a high value on formal train-
      ing for public administration. An agreement
      with the U.S. in 1956 to train civil servants
      under the auspices of the University of
      Southern California helped rectify the situa-
      tion, as did the establishment of a series
      of training institutes in the country.
      Nevertheless, serious training problems re-
      main. Among these are (1) an absence of
      linkages between training and career plan-
      ning; (2) lack of incentives for officers to

take training; (c) lack of penetration of
training to lower ranks of the service.

147. Abdel-Rahim, Muddathir. "Training: The
    Sudanese Experience." *Philippine Journal
    of Public Administration*, 17, 2 (April 1973),
    210-226.

    Sudanese administrative training programs
    have had three primary aims: (1) elimination
    of Egyptian influences; (2) achievement of
    nationalism; (3) improvement of education.
    "Sudanization" of the bureaucracy created
    problems in efficiency and effectiveness, and
    led to the establishment of various institutes.
    These have helped but have not solved the
    problem completely.

148. Adams, J.S. "Soviet Inspectors General: An
    Expanding Role." *Soviet Studies*, 20, 1
    (July 1968), 106-111.

    Discusses organization and function of
    People's Control Committees of the Soviet
    Union. Describes three main characteristics:
    (1) mass participation; (2) systematic effort
    to perform activities in public view; (3)
    educational role. Argues that fulfillment
    of these three functions will help construct
    the model "Soviet man" of the 1970's.

149. Adedeji, Adebayo, ed. *Problems and Techniques
    of Administrative Training in Africa.*
    Ibadan, Nigeria: Caxton Press, 1969.

    Eleven selections on various aspects of
    administrative training, derived from a 1965
    conference at the University of Ife. Problem-
    focused rather than country-focused, with sole
    emphasis on training for development adminis-
    tration.

150. Adu, A.L. *The Civil Service in New African
    States.* New York: Praeger, 1965.

Descriptive outline of civil service systems in Africa in immediate post-colonial period. Treats structure and control of civil services, recruitment and training, problems of "Africanization," labor relations, and financial affairs. Appendices on salary structures and organizational charts.

151. Akinsanya, Adeoye. "The Machinery of Government During the Military Regime in Nigeria." *International Review of Administrative Sciences*, 42, 4 (1976), 357-361.

Identifies a centralizing tendency in Nigerian military rule which contradicts the federal nature of the state. This is attributed to the unified and hierarchical nature of the military, as well as the orientation of high-level bureaucrats. Analyzes the activities of the military regime from 1968 in executive, legislative, and judicial spheres.

152. Aktan, Tahir. "The New State Personnel Department in Turkey." *International Review of Administrative Sciences*, 33, 2 (1967), 151-154.

Prior to 1960, there was little central direction given to public personnel policy in Turkey; only minimal coordination was provided by the Ministry of Finance. The establishment of the state Personnel Department has provided direction in this area. This department is responsible for classifying positions, reviewing manpower requirements, maintaining records, and other related tasks. The problem now is that the Department is understaffed and has only advisory authority.

153. Allison, Gary D. "Public Servants and Public Interests in Contemporary Japan." *Asian Survey*, 20, 10 (October 1980), 1048-1068.

Discusses problems of public employee labor
relations in Japanese municipal government.
Begins with a case study of a Tokyo suburb.
Major argument is that conflicts between labor
and government will increase greatly in years
to come.

154. Al-Teraifi, Al-Agab A. "Promotion in the
     Sudanese Civil Service." Public Personnel
     Management, 9, 1 (January/February 1980),
     19-24.

     Examines promotion and advancement policies
     in Sudanese civil service. Demonstrates weak-
     nesses, such as (1) greater emphasis on
     seniority, (2) absence of uniform standards,
     and (3) predominance of ascriptive over
     achievement criteria. Also analyzes limita-
     tions of system introduced in 1973 to remedy
     these deficiencies.

155. Al-Teraifi, Al-Agab A. "Recent Administrative
     Reforms in the Sudan." International Review
     of Administrative Sciences, 45, 2 (1979),
     136-146.

     Discusses changes fostered by the Ministry
     of Public Service and Administrative Reform
     since its establishment in 1971. Credits
     this agency with providing coordinated
     institutional support to various administra-
     tive reforms.

156. Ankomah, Kofi. "Reflections on Administra-
     tive Reform in Ghana." International Re-
     view of Administrative Sciences, 36, 4
     (1970), 299-303.

     Reviews the operation and recommendations
     of civil service investigatory commission in
     Ghana following the overthrow of Kwame
     Nkrumah. Criticizes the Commission's neglect
     of key civil service failings, including lack
     of coordination, poor personnel practices,
     and under-utilization of specialists.

157. Armstrong, John A. *The European Administrative Elite.* Princeton: Princeton University Press, 1973.

Major comparative study of the evolution of elite administrative roles in Britain, France, Russia, and Prussia. A principal focus is the explanation for "development interventionism" on the part of administrators; case studies of railroad building are used to explicate. Chapters are generally organized to follow the course of administrative role socialization-- from family through educational institutions to career patterns.

158. Armstrong, John A. "Old-Regime Administrative Elites." *International Review of Administrative Sciences*, 38, 1 (1972), 21-40.

Historical analysis of French, Russian, and Prussian administrative elites, with special attention to elites' relationship to process of modernization; a precursor to and condensation of item 157. Treats social class, recruitment, and socialization of elites.

159. Armstrong, John A. "Old-Regime Governors: Bureaucratic and Patrimonial Attributes." *Comparative Studies in Society and History,* 14, 1 (January 1972), 2-29.

Poses the question: to what extent did governors in premodern societies resemble modern bureaucratic officials? Uses concept of "bureaucratic regression" (move toward patrimonial characteristics) to discuss question, drawing on case material from Russian and French history. Finds greater regression among French <u>intendants</u> than Russian <u>gubernators</u>.

160. Armstrong, John A. "Sources of Administrative Behavior: Some Soviet and Western European Comparisons." *American Political Science*

Review, 59, 3 (September 1965), 643-655.

Western European and Soviet administrative
behavior is similar in that they both depart
from hierarchical command principles in certain areas, rest on informal relationships,
persisting associations between old classmates,
and the importance of performance criteria as
motivations. Differs in several important
respects. Traces patterns of differences to
either ideology or to rapidity of economic
development.

161   Armstrong, John A. *The Soviet Bureaucratic
      Elite*. New York: Praeger, 1959.

Analytical study of top-level Soviet administrators with case material drawn primarily
from Ukraine. Describes who administrators are
in terms of social background, and how they
rose to elite positions. Finds great diversity
in composition as well as greatly increased
educational levels. Behavioral features of the
elite are examined in two special case studies:
the expansion of Soviet rule to the Western
Ukraine and the German invasion of 1941.

*   Bachrach, Samuel B. and J. Lawrence French.
      "Role Allocation Processes in Public Bureau-
      cracies." Cited as item 74.

162. Baker, Colin. "The Administrative Service of
      Malawi." *Journal of Modern African Studies*,
      10, 4 (December 1972), 543-560.

Focuses on the Africanization of the Malawi
Civil Service. Treats period from early pre-
independence years to 1970. Includes date on
growth of service and changes in composition.
Transition has been relatively smooth, with
European expatriates allowed to stay until
they voluntarily wished to retire.

163. Barad, Miryam. "Women as Managers in Israel." *Public Administration in Israel and Abroad,* 1966, Volume 7 (1966), 78-87.

Describes factors which prevent or hinder advancement of women to managerial levels in Israel. Concludes that status of women managers in Israel is similar to that in the United States and Britain. Argues that lack of status is a result of a vicious cycle involving women's interests and aspirations, attitudes of society, and environmental conditions.

164. Barber, Laurence L. "The Revision of the Somali Civil Service." *International Review of Administrative Sciences,* 32, 2 (1966), 134-144.

Historical summary of Somali administration, followed by detailed examination of the structure of the civil service. Includes a breakdown of positions by ministry, methods of recruitment and salary systems. Concludes with a discussion of recent administrative reforms.

165. Barnett, A. Doak. "Social Stratification and Aspects of Personnel Management in the Communist Chinese Bureaucracy." *China Quarterly,* 28 (October/December 1966), 8-39.

Discusses the tensions between bureaucratization and political control of Chinese administration in context of a case study of a single ministry. Outlines salary and job rank systems, and treats conflicts between "old" and "new" cadres. Concludes with description of career management and mobility and the impact on lives of individual bureaucrats.

166. Bashir, Iskandar. "Training for the Public Sector in Lebanon." *International Review of Administrative Sciences,* 40, 4 (1974), 359-365.

Following a brief history of administrative
training in Lebanon prior to independence,
examines the programs conducted by the National
Institute of Public Administration and Development. Identifies several major problems with
training, including lack of staff, curricular
rigidity, heterogeneity of trainees and lack of
motivation.

*   Baum, Edward. "Recent Administrative Reform
in Local Government in Northern Nigeria."
Cited as item 558.

167. Beaumont, P.B. "The Obligation of the Government as Employer in the British Civil Service." *Public Administration* (London), 56
(Spring 1978), 13-24.

Brief historical review of public sector
wage policy in Britain, leading to a discussion
of contemporary government efforts to restrain
pay. Argues that the two operating assumptions
behind this policy--namely that public sector
wages pace private sector pay and that the
government is in a stronger position to restrain excessive wages--are flawed and need to
be revised.

168. Ben-Dor, Gabriel. "Corruption, Institutionali-
zation, and Political Development: the
Revisionist Theses Revisited." *Comparative
Political Studies*, 7, 1 (April 1974), 63-83.

Examines three "revisionist" schools of
corruption--the institutionalists, the func-
tional-integrationists, and the market-economic
developmentalists--in the context of developed
politics. Argues that the first is the most
applicable at this stage, though its explanation of the roots of corruption is suspect.
None of the revisionist theories has adequately accounted for changes in the character of
corruption across the stages of development.

* Bent, Frederick. "The Turkish Bureaucracy as
  an Agent of Change." Cited as item 337.

169. Bhambhri, C.P. "Socialization of IAS Officers:
     Training and Milieu." *International Review
     of Administrative Sciences*, 38, 1 (1972), 61-
     71.

     Reports survey of eighty young Indian
     Administrative Service officers tracked through
     initial two year period of service. Examines
     backgrounds, attitudes toward their training
     and views about political leaders and adminis-
     trative supervisors. Includes thirteen tables.

170. Blume, Stuart S. and Elizabeth Chennells.
     "Professional Civil Servants: A Study in the
     Sociology of Public Administration." *Public
     Administration* (London), 53 (Summer 1975),
     111-132.

     Draws on interviews with fifty specialists
     in British bureaucracy to present an overall
     sociological picture. Analyzes perceived sig-
     nificance of work, task involvement, pro-
     fessional identification, and career aspira-
     tions.

171 Boise, William B. "The French National School
     of Administration and the Education of Career
     Executives." *Public Personnel Review*, 30, 1
     (January 1969), 31-35.

     General overview of Ecole Nationale
     d'Administration (ENA). Includes some data on
     graduates, including ministries of initial
     assignment. Makes case for development of a
     similar institution in the United States.

172. Braibanti, Ralph. "Reflections on Bureaucratic
     Corruption." *Public Administration* (London),
     40 (Winter 1962), 357-372.

Discusses twelve "partial explanations" of administrative corruption--from personal venality to social immorality--and ten possible immediate steps that can be taken as correctives. Concludes that there is no single cause of corruption. The solution lies in multiple remedies at all levels of action.

173. Brown, R.G.S. "Fulton and Morals." *Public Administration* (London), 49 (Summer 1971), 185-195.

Reports survey of attitudes toward career of 101 recent Civil Service entrants in the immediate post-Fulton Report period. Comparisons are made in the discussion with similar surveys conducted by others for earlier cohorts. Levels of satisfaction were found to be relatively high, though criticisms were voiced over issues like promotion and intellectual challenge.

174. Brugger, William. *Democracy and Organization in the Chinese Industrial Enterprise.* Cambridge: Cambridge University Press, 1975.

Examines the immediate post-Revolution period (to 1953) to ascertain what sort of authority patterns the Chinese communists established in factories. Begins with a comparison of Chinese, Soviet and Japanese models of industrial management. Discusses the effects of political environment in early 1950's on management patterns. Especially interested in tension between administrative rationalization and worker participation, and in Chinese reaction to the imposed Soviet model of management.

175. Caiden, Gerald. *Administrative Reform.* Chicago: Aldine Publishing Co., 1969.

Attempts to define "administrative reform" as a new subfield. Administrative reform is "the artificial inducement of administrative

transformation against resistance." Discusses
relationships between administrative theory and
administrative reform, and social change and
administrative reform. Includes limited efforts
to hypothesize about causes and consequences of
reform.

176. Caiden, Gerald. *The Commonwealth Bureaucracy*.
     Melbourne: Melbourne University Press, 1967.

     Comprehensive examination of Australian
     federal personnel policies and practices. Four
     major headings include: Profile of the Common-
     wealth Bureaucracy, Personnel Authorities in
     the Commonwealth Service, Personnel Administra-
     tion in the Commonwealth Service, and Emerging
     Problems. Includes detailed statistical in-
     formation.

177. Caiden, Gerald. *Israel's Administrative Cul-
     ture*. Berkeley: Institute of Governmental
     Studies, 1970.

     General history of Israeli public administra-
     tion written around the theme of "administra-
     tive culture," which refers to "accepted ways
     in which the members of society go about get-
     ting things done." Treats questions of policy
     formulation, planning, organization, budgeting
     and innovation. Identifies specific elements
     in Israeli administrative culture, including
     lack of specialization and organizational
     rigidity.

178. Caiden, Gerald. "Prospects for Administrative
     Reform in Israel." *Public Administration*
     (London), 46 (Spring 1968), 25-44.

     Attempts to explain the paradox of great
     administrative adaptability to environmental
     challenge and change in the absence of formal
     administrative reform. Reviews the history of
     Israeli public administration and discusses
     some of its structural weaknesses. Argues
     that reform is needed to permit continued

adaptation, but suggests that Israelis will avoid extreme action.

179. Camp, Roderic Al. "The Cabinet and the Técnico in Mexico and the U.S." *Journal of Comparative Administration,* 3, 1 (August 1971), 188-214.

    Finds that in Mexico, as in the U.S., an increasing proportion of political and administrative elites are marked by technical backgrounds. This is especially true for agencies dealing with economic and social problems.

180. Campbell, Colin and C.J. Szablowski. *The Superbureaucrats.* Toronto: Gage Publishing, Ltd., 1979.

    Detailed examination of elite administrators in Canadian central government. Based on interviews with 92 officials (out of a universe of 102) holding positions at the level of director or above in five central government ministries. Deals with recruitment, roles, accountability, and performance. Identifies weaknesses of the system, including the need for better training and better policy advice for the Prime Minister's Office.

181. Carson, John J. "Bilingualism in the Public Service." *Canadian Public Administration,* 15, 2 (Summer 1972), 190-193.

    Chairman of Canadian Public Service Commission sets forth rationale and objectives of the bilingualism program. Although progress has been made in some areas, particularly in lower level jobs, work still needs to be done to make the executive offices more representative of Francophones.

182. Carson, John. "What's Happened to Glassco?"
     Public Personnel Review 26, 2 (April 1965),
     70-72.

     Outlines progress in implementation of the
     recommendations of the Royal Commission on
     Government Organization in the Canadian public
     service. Summarizes proposals. Concludes that
     substantial work needs to be done, especially
     in the areas of the role of the Civil Service
     Commission, public service integration, finan-
     cial decentralization, and productivity im-
     provement.

183. Caulcott, T.H. and P. Mountfield, "Decentrali-
     zed Administration in Sweden." *Public
     Administration* (London), 52 (Spring 1974),
     41-53.

     In part because of the enthusiasms of the
     Fulton Report, British commentators have looked
     wistfully at the Swedish administrative sys-
     tem, with its purportedly smooth-functioning,
     decentralized, and autonomous public boards.
     After examining the separations of powers,
     the state of ministerial responsibility, and
     the relationships between ministries, staff,
     boards and parliament, concludes that the
     Swedish model (a) does not conform to the
     popular myth and (b) is not suitable for trans-
     plant to Britain.

184. Cervantes del Rio, Hugo. "Public Administra-
     tion in Mexico." *International Review of
     Administrative Sciences,* 40, 1 (1974), 1-7.

     Brief structural description of Mexican
     public administration by the Secretary to the
     President. Includes outline of proposed re-
     forms and speculation on future of Mexican
     administration.

185. Chapman, Brian. *The Profession of Government.*
     London: George Allen and Unwin, 1959.

Broad ranging analysis of recruitment, training, conditions of service, and forms of
administrative control in continental Western
European public bureaucracies. Includes coverage of Belgium, Denmark, France, Germany, Italy,
the Netherlands, Portugal, Spain, Sweden, and
Switzerland.

186. Chapman, Leslie. *Your Disobedient Servant*.
London: Chatto and Windus, 1978.

Attack on waste and inefficiency in the British Civil Service by a former senior administrator. First section describes how some
economies came to be made in the Ministry of
Public Buildings and Works under Chapman's
guidance; second section chronicles reactions
to those economies, while third concludes with
recommendations for change. Book is of
interest in part because of the public outcry
it generated on publication in Britain.

187. Chapman, Richard A. "Administrative Reform in
Saudi Arabia." *Journal of Administration
Overseas*, 13, 2 (April 1974), 332-347.

Deals mainly with manpower problems (speci-
fically shortages) in Saudi Arabia. Provides
overview of Saudi political and economic systems. One of the main Saudi administrative
problems is bureaucratic over-employment, which
stems from the government's efforts to dis-
tribute oil wealth through salaries.

188. Chapman, Richard A. "The Fulton Report: A
Summary." *Public Administration* (London),
46 (Winter 1968), 443-451.

As the title indicates, summarizes Report of
the Committee on the Civil Service (the Fulton
Report). Good chapter by chapter synopses
of findings and recommendations.

189. Chapman, Richard A. "Reducing the Public Sector: The Thatcher Government's Approach."
Policy Studies Journal 9, 8 (Special #4,
1980-81), 1152-1163.

The ideology of the Conservative government
of Margaret Thatcher and the underlying patterns of administrative change in Britain have
become intertwined. Reviews philosophy and
approach of Thatcher government and cites
examples of recent attempts to reduce public
sector spending. Suggests that traditional
reformist approach to administrative matters
is being interspersed with some radical political departures under the Tories.

190. Chapman, Richard A. "The Vehicle and General
Affair: Some Reflections for Public Adminis-
tration in Britain." *Public Administration*
(London), 51 (Autumn 1973), 273-290.

Analyzes some questions of professional conduct and administrative process in the context
of the Vehicle and General case, a scandal
involving the failure of a major automobile
insurance company in 1971, in which civil service negligence or misconduct was alleged.
After recounting the facts of the case, argues
that it raises questions about administrative
accountability--in particular the extent to
which civil servants have become more account-
able (unfortunately) than ministers.

191. Christoph, James B. "A Comparative View:
Administrative Secrecy in Britain." *Public
Administration Review*, 35, 1 (January/February
1975), 23-32.

Traces roots of administrative secrecy in
Britain to general political structures and
attitudes, and the doctrine of ministerial
responsibility. Discusses "Estacode" (conduct
manual for the Civil Service) and the Official
Secrets Act. Sees some opening in the wall of
secrecy in recent years.

192. Cicco, John A. "Japan's Administrative Elite." *International Review of Administrative Sciences*, 4 (October-December 1975), 379-384.

    Reports the results of a survey of 56 Japanese higher civil servants designed to ascertain self-perceptions of the requirements for elite membership. The four most important factors identified in order of importance were: (1) attendance at prestigious public universities; (2) continuous assignment in one ministry; (3) legal education; and (4) good professional contacts. Notes strains on elite cohesion arising from social, economic and technological change.

193. Crispo, John. "Collective Bargaining in the Public Service." *Canadian Public Administration*, 16, 1 (Spring 1973), 1-13.

    Overview of Canadian public sector labor relations. Describes relevant statutes and discusses nature of bargaining units, allowable scope of bargaining, and special problems for labor and management. Concludes with a consideration of compulsory arbitration. Finds this means of dispute settlement dangerous, something that should be used only when all else fails.

194. Dana Montaño, Salvador M. "Rol del Estado y de la Administración Pública." *International Review of Administrative Sciences*, 41, 1 (1975), 61-66.

    Looks historically at the relationship between administration and three forms of the state--the Constitutional, the Law and the Welfare--in Argentina. Changes in the nature of the state have carried implications for the type of training necessary; especially in recent days, there has been a de-emphasis on law narrowly defined.

195. Darbel, A. and D. Schnapper. "Les Structures
de l'Administration Française." *International Review of Administrative Sciences,*
40, 4 (1974), 335-349.

Overview of major characteristics of French
administration. Sections on: implications of
public service monopoly; mechanisms of control;
and administrative attitudes.

196. Dodd, C.H. "Administrative Reform in Turkey."
Public Administration (London), 43 (Spring
1965), 71-83.

Discusses efforts of an administrative reform commission, established in 1962, to re-
assess the structure of the Turkish central
administration. Provides background information on the Turkish administrative system.
Argues for greater attention to problems of
recruitment and training.

197. Dodd, C.H. "Recruitment of Administrative
Class." *Public Administration* (London), 45
(Spring 1967), 55-80.

Reports research on educational backgrounds
of successful and unsuccessful candidates for
appointment to the Administrative Class. Includes twelve tables giving breakdowns of
secondary schools and universities attended,
class of degree, subject of degree, and type
of qualifying examination. Concludes that
Oxford and Cambridge students have a competitive edge.

198. Doig, Alan. "The Machinery of Government and
the Growth of Government Bodies." *Public
Administration* (London), 57 (Autumn 1979),
309-332.

Surveys the rise of semi-autonomous governmental bodies in Britain. Provides data on
numbers, relationships to existing departments,

and staff size. Suggests some reasons for
their explosive growth, and counsels a
reassertion of representative controls.

199. Dresang, Dennis. "Ethnic Politics, Representative Bureaucracy, and Development Administration: The Zambian Case." *American Political
Science Review*, 68, 4 (December 1974), 1605-
1617.

Provides evidence from Zambian bureaucracy
that administrative behavior is not primarily
a function of social, ethnic or cultural factors. Argues that main determinants of
behavior found in bureaucrat's perception of
what must be done to advance career. Although
this suggests that "representative bureaucracies" will not necessarily act in a manner
reflective of social cleavages, representation
is important for symbolic reasons in frag-
mented societies.

200. Edwards, Claude. "Federal Employee Relations
Up North: The Canadian Experience." *Public
Personnel Management*, 4, 6 (November/Decem-
ber 1975), 305-371.

Article by president of the Canadian Public
Service Alliance provides overview of contemporary Canadian public sector labor relations. Discusses Public Service Staff Relations Act of 1967, which established framework for collective bargaining. Focuses on
perceived limitations and present difficulties
in bargaining.

201. Finlay, Ian. "La Fonction Publique." *International Review of Administrative Sciences*,
34, 1 (1968), 25-81.

Overview of the Irish Civil Service. Discusses legislative basis, size, parliamentary
oversight, and the role of the Department of
Finance as the central civil service ministry.
Some material on budget preparation is also
included, as is information on classification,

recruitment, and the role of the Irish civil
servant.

202. Fonseca Pimentel, A. "La Administración de
     Personal en América Latina." *International
     Review of Administrative Sciences,* 32, 3
     (1966) 197-210.

     Capsule summaries of personnel administration
     systems in five Latin American countries:
     Brazil, Costa Rica, Panama, Colombia and
     Ecuador. Includes information on recruitment,
     career systems, training and salary provisions.

203. François, Aimé. "Aspects de la Fonction
     Publique en Belgique." *International Review
     of Administrative Sciences,* 45, 4 (1979),
     312-320.

     Describes history and structure of the career
     civil service in Belgian central government.
     Argues that politicization within the adminis-
     tration is the most important current problem.

204. Franko, Ivan. "Federal Administrative Agen-
     cies of Yugoslavia--Their Role, Position,
     and Organization." *International Review of
     Administrative Sciences,* 42, 2 (1976), 145-
     152.

     Describes the functions, authority and
     management of Yugoslav federal agencies under
     the 1974 Constitution.

205. Fry, Geoffrey K. "Civil Service Salaries in
     the Post-Priestly Era, 1956-1972," *Public
     Administration* (London), 52 (Autumn 1974),
     319-333.

     Following the report of the Priestly Com-
     mission in 1955, the primary mechanism for
     determining administrative pay has been the
     Civil Service Pay Research Unit, which is re-
     sponsible for doing comparability studies.

The advent of this system has allowed the
majority of mid-level civil servants in
Britain to fare well, although lower level
administrators were less generously compensated. Includes three tables of pay data,
broken down by class, year, and percentage
increase.

206. Fry, Geoffrey K. "Some Weaknesses in the
     Fulton Report on the British Home Civil
     Service." *Political Studies*, 17, 3 (1969),
     484-494.

     Criticizes the narrowness of the charge of
     the Fulton Committee (for instance, excluding
     investigating the doctrine of ministerial
     responsibility). Although the Committee made
     some good recommendations, others were un-
     acceptable. The Report was weakened by a lack
     of an historical perspective and an unwilling-
     ness to quantify its proposals. Issue is also
     taken with the Committee's recommendations on
     service structure and recruitment.

207. Fry, Geoffrey K. *Statesmen in Disguise.*
     London: Macmillan, 1969.

     One of the most detailed extant analyses of
     the origin and operation of the British
     Administrative Class. Covers period from
     1853 to 1966. Discusses methods of recruit-
     ment and training and the relationship between
     members of Administrative, Executive, and
     Clerical Classes, as well as the role of
     specialists. Detailed statistical appendices
     included. Concludes with observations about
     the Fulton Report.

208. Gammon, Geoffrey and David Young. "The
     Ministry of Defence's Review of Personnel
     Management in the Administration Group and
     its Consequences." *Public Administration*
     (London), 57 (Autumn 1979), 271-285.

Between 1977 and 1979, the British Ministry of Defence began to implement basic changes in personnel management policy toward the higher administrative staff. The main thrust was to move career development closer to a "functional" model to make better use of specialists.

209. Garcia-Zamor, Jean-Claude. "An Ecological Approach to Administrative Reform: The Brazilian Case." *International Review of Administrative Sciences*, 35, 4 (1969), 315-320.

The inability of the Brazilian bureaucracy to meet the tasks of development cannot be successfully addressed by narrowly focused administrative reforms such as changes in training or personnel systems. Administrative inefficiency is mainly a reflection of ecological factors, including growth or urban population, rigid social structure, and military action. Real administrative reform must address these environmental problems.

210. Gazier, Francois. "L'Ecole Nationale d'Administration: Apparences et Réalitiés." *International Review of Administrative Sciences*, 31, 1 (1965), 31-34.

Brief overview of ENA and its activities by the school's director. Notes that ENA is unlike universities in physical plant and style of instruction. All of the teaching staff, save one person, is part-time. Training at the post-graduate level is equally divided between theoretical and practical work. Student motivation is very high since placement depends directly on rank in class. ENA has sole responsibility for recruiting and training members of the prestigious Grand Corps. All students have civil service status, are paid while at school, and must agree to serve the state for ten years after their course of 28 months. Four basic subjects are studied: (1) public administration and administrative law; (2) economics and finance; (3) social science; (4) international relations. No in-service training is provided.

211. Geare, A.J. "Collective Bargaining and Arbitration." *New Zealand Journal of Public Administration*, 39, 2 (September 1977), 1-5.

Takes issue with the "truism" that collective bargaining is superior to arbitration. Illustrates arguments by reference to New Zealand experience, and draws contrasts with Australia. Preference for either method of dispute settlement is a matter of value judgment and situational factors.

212. Gibbons, David S. and Zakaria Haji Ahmad. "Politics and Selection for the Higher Civil Service in New States: The Malaysian Example." *Journal of Comparative Administration*, 3, 3 (November 1971), 330-348.

Despite the operation of a quota system, ethnic Malays remain underrepresented in the higher civil service in Malaysia, although their numbers in the overall service exceed their proportions of the population. This overrepresentation overall has helped keep elite recruitment from becoming a political issue, and has thus contributed to the effectiveness of the service.

213. Gillender, K. and R. Mair. "Generalist Administrators and Professional Engineers: Some Developments Since the Fulton Report." *Public Administration* (London), 58 (Autumn 1980), 333-356.

Traces career patterns of engineers in three British ministries to determine effect of Fulton reforms. Progress toward resolving specialist-generalist tensions have been uneven at best. Engineers experience less mobility than their Administrative Group counterparts.

214. Globerson, Arye. "A Profile of the Bureaucra-
     tic Elite in Israel." *Public Personnel
     Management*, 2, 1 (January/February 1973),
     9-15.

     Describes characteristics of elite Israeli
     public administrators. Based on interviews
     with 294 senior officials in 18 ministries.
     Finds that the average administrator is male,
     fifty years of age, and a university graduate
     of East European origin.

215. Glueck, William F. and Dragoljub Kavran.
     "The Yugoslav Management System." *Manage-
     ment International Review*, 11, 2-3 (1971),
     3-17.

     After describing some of the economic, poli-
     tical and social background of Yugoslavia,
     describes Yugoslav self-management system.
     Provides productivity data, and argues that
     this system has led to higher output. Con-
     cludes with a comparison of participation in
     Yugoslavia with systems in America and Europe.

216. Godchot, Jacques E. "La Formation Permanente
     des Cadres Supérieurs de la Fonction Publique
     in France." *International Review of
     Administrative Sciences*, 36, 1 (1970), 18-21.

     Describes ongoing training for higher French
     civil servants, which has been mandatory since
     1945. Much of this is done through the Center
     for Higher Administrative Studies, an affiliate
     of ENA. Unfortunately, very few civil servants
     are willing to attend the classes, since there
     is no guarantee of material benefit.

217. Goodnow, Henry Frank. *The Civil Service of
     Pakistan: Bureaucracy in a New Nation*. New
     Haven: Yale, 1964.

     General study of public administration in
     Pakistan. Major emphasis is on the evolution
     and role of the Civil Service of Pakistan (CSP).

Discusses CSP relationships with other actors, recruitment and training questions, and pay and assignment systems. Concludes that while a strong CSP is essential to Pakistani development, it is important to prevent bureaucratic dominance by mooring to a plural society.

218. Goslin, R.C. "Development and Training of Senior Administrators in the U.K. Civil Service." *International Review of Administrative Sciences*, 45, 1 (1979), 6-20.

Discusses current issues and problems in training programs for higher civil servants in Britain, including lack of evaluation, theoretical v. practical approaches, OD v. university training. A major problem is perceptions of training: is it a preface to promotion or a dumping ground?

219. Graham, L.S. *Civil Service Reform in Brazil: Principles Versus Practice.* Austin and London: University of Texas Press, 1968.

Examines efforts of Brazilian leaders to create a modern, American-style personnel system. Little success was forthcoming in meeting this objective. This has been due to political factors, in particular excessive decentralization of authority coupled with a basic lack of political consensus.

220. Granick, David. "Managerial Incentives in the USSR and in Western Firms." *Journal of Comparative Administration*, 5, 2 (August 1973), 169-199.

Poor economic performance in the USSR is due more to poor managerial incentives than to economic centralization per se. Soviet theory is still at the stage of Taylorism in its emphasis on managerial bonuses. Soviet leaders seem not fully to recognize this problem and have eschewed more Western techniques to induce managerial innovation and performance.

221. Green, R.L, M.R. Palmer and T.J. Sanger. "Why
     They Leave--A Study of Public Service Resig-
     nations and Morale." *New Zealand Journal of
     Public Administration,* 30, 1 (September 1967),
     17-38.

     Examines reasons for staff turnover in New
     Zealand Public Service. Reports results of
     survey of 134 permanent civil servants re-
     signing in a two month period in 1961. Most
     reasons given had to do with the nature of the
     job, rather than with monetary considerations.
     Offers several recommendations to personnel
     officials to deal with turnover problems.

222. Groves, Roderick T. "Administrative Reform
     and the Politics of Reform: The Case of
     Venezuela." *Public Administration Review,*
     27, 5 (December 1967), 436-445.

     Seeks to explain the failures of a major
     program of administrative reform in Venezuela
     in 1958, which was personnel oriented. Lack
     of success is attributed mainly to the unwill-
     ingness of the reformers to understand the
     destabilizing effects of a merit-based civil
     service on the regime.

223. Hager, L. Michael. "Bureaucratic Corruption in
     India: Legal Control of Maladministration."
     Comparative Political Studies, 6, 2 (July
     1973), 197-220.

     A general study of administrative corruption
     in India. Focuses on two main questions: "Why
     corruption?" and "What can be done?" One of
     the difficulties in rooting out corruption is
     the fact that it takes so many forms, legal
     and administrative controls have little effec-
     tiveness. Concludes that broad social reforms,
     such as freer press, political maturation, and
     ministerial examples of integrity are needed.

224. Hamaoui, E. "La Fonction Publique en Afghani-
     stan." *International Review of Administra-
     tive Sciences,* 39, 3 (1973), 259-264.

     General description of Afghani civil service
     system, which resembles in form those of con-
     tinental Europe. Outlines recruitment proce-
     dures, conditions of employment, career system,
     pay and retirement provisions. Focuses partic-
     ularly on 1971 revision of 1944 Basic Law.

225. Hamilton, Stuart and Sue Hamilton. "The Royal
     Commission on Australian Government Adminis-
     tration: A Descriptive Overview." *Australian
     Journal of Public Administration,* 354
     (December 1976), 303-310.

     Brief review of main points of Commission's
     report released in 1976. Report discusses
     inadequacies of administration and outlines
     prescriptions for reform, including greater
     decentralization of power.

226. Hanf, Kenneth. "Administrative Developments
     in East and West Germany: Stirrings of
     Reform." *Political Studies,* 21, 1 (1973),
     35-44.

     Despite great regime differences, parallel
     administrative developments have occurred in
     East and West Germany. In each country,
     efforts are being made to rationalize adminis-
     tration and make it more adaptive. However,
     the political institutions and values of the
     two societies have produced and will continue
     to produce differences. One should not assume
     that there is a single imperative that will
     produce one most rational form of administra-
     tion for all countries.

227. Harris, John S. and Thomas V. Garcia. "The
     Permanent Secretaries: Britain's Top
     Administrators." *Public Administration
     Review,* 26, 1 (March 1966), 31-44.

Reviews the role of the permanent secretary
in Britain. Although the formal responsibilities of this office have not changed apprecia-
bly in over 100 years, the educational and
social backgrounds of those who occupy the
posts have.

228. Headey, Bruce. "The Civil Service as an Elite
in Britain and Germany." *International
Review of Administrative Sciences*, 38, 1
(1972), 41-48.

Report on a 1969 conference at Reading University on problems of administration in
Western Europe. Examines various conceptions
of the proper roles of civil service elites
in Britain and West Germany. Notes congruence
of views on issues such as skills required for
the civil service and methods of recruitment.

229. Helin, Jean-Claude. "Les Agents Temporaires
dans la Fonction Publique Tunisienne."
*International Review of Administrative
Sciences*, 43, 3 (1977), 205-222.

Discusses the legal problems of temporary
staff in Tunisia, estimated in 1970 to account
for half of all employees. Efforts have since
been made to ensure that recruitment of
temporary workers will be the exception rather
than the rule.

230. Hodgetts, J.E. *The Canadian Public Service*.
Toronto: University of Toronto Press, 1973.

Historical survey of Canadian public
administration from 1867 to 1970. Part One
outlines the context or environment of
Canadian public administration, with chapters
on social, political and legal systems. Part
Two devotes six chapters to questions of
departmental design and organizational structure. The third part focuses on relatively
contemporary problems in Canadian public service, such as the role of the Treasury Board,

the position of the Public Service Commission, and so forth.

231. Hoetjes, B.J.S. "Secrecy and Publicity in a Parliamentary Democracy--The Case of the Netherlands." *Indian Journal of Public Administration*, 25, 4 (October/December 1979), 1016-1024.

Discusses the reasons for and laws regulating administrative secrecy in the Netherlands. The Netherlands is now one of the few countries in the world where publicity has a firm legal foundation. Includes summarized text of 1978 Law on Access to Official Information.

232. Hopkins, Jack. "Comparative Observations on Peruvian Bureaucracy." *Journal of Comparative Administration*, 1, 3 (November 1969), 301-320.

Analyzes data on backgrounds, mobility and attitudes of senior Peruvian public executives. Based on sample of 380 officials of 9 ministries and several autonomous organizations. Draws comparisons with the U.S. Finds Peruvian bureaucrats are more autonomous from legislative control, more hierarchically rigid, less concerned with popular consent, less professionalized, and less innovative, among other things.

233. Hopkins, Jack. *The Government Executive of Modern Peru.* Gainesville: University of Florida Press, 1967.

Empirical analysis of the backgrounds, origins, mobility, and attitudes of a sample of senior government officials in Peru. See item 232.

234. Huddleston, Mark W. "Comparative Perspectives on Administrative Ethics." *Public Personnel*

Management, 10, 1 (1981), 67-76.

Identifies three major patterns of administrative ethics--polity-based, statist, and
transcendent--and discusses why they develop,
persist and change. Illustrates with examples
drawn from major administrative systems,
including Britain, France, Germany, and Japan.

235. Hughes, H.D. "The Settlement of Disputes in
the Public Service." *Public Administration*
(London), 46 (Spring 1968), 45-62.

Wideranging comparative analysis of theories
and mechanisms of government-labor relations.
Discusses "barriers of legalism," questions of
sovereignty, arbitration, and other forms of
conciliation.

236. Ilchman, Warren F. "The Unproductive Study
of Productivity: Public Administration in
Developing Nations." *Comparative Political
Studies*, 1, 2 (July 1968), 227-250.

In an effort "to improve the statesman's
choices," sets forth a framework for studying
productivity in developing countries. Current
scholarly knowledge is generally useless, if
not harmful, for policy-makers. Derides
academics for subscribing to a "religion of
development" devoid of empirical content,
and "intellectual colonialism."

237. Johnson, Chalmers. "The Reemployment of
Retired Government Bureaucrats in Japanese
Big Business." *Asian Survey*, 14, 11
(November 1974), 953-965.

Explores actual movement of public officials
to private sector and public attitudes toward
same. One major reason for transfer is early
retirement from government, normally in one's
early fifties, although this is mainly a post-
war phenomenon. This practice, called

amakudari, has now become well institutionalized.

238. Jumelle, Leon. "La Reforme Administrative en
     Zaire." *International Review of Administra-
     tive Sciences*, 40, 2 (1974), 171-182.

     Lists several major administrative reforms
     that have been underway in Zaire since 1972,
     including: (1) reduction in size of senior
     staff; (2) executive reorganization; (3)
     decentralization of personnel functions; (4)
     reorganized field servcies; and (5) new rules
     governing the conduct of civil servants.

239. Kardelj, Edvard. "Socialist Self-Management
     in Yugoslavia." *International Review of
     Administrative Sciences*, 42, 2 (1976), 103-
     110.

     Argues that Yugoslav self-management resolves
     the dilemma of maintaining human freedom and
     dignity in an age of industrial concentration
     and centralization.

240. Kearney, R.N. and R.L. Harris. "Bureaucracy
     and Environment in Ceylon." *Journal of
     Commonwealth Political Studies*, 2, 3
     (November 1964), 253-266.

     Traces the impact of the social, cultural
     and political environment of Ceylon on the
     Ceylonese bureaucracy. Despite lingering
     influences of caste and commune, a major
     problem in Ceylonese administration is
     bureaucratic isolation from society. Western-
     ized elites are out of touch with nationalist
     sentiments. Moreover, the disproportionate
     representation of minorities in the bureau-
     cracy make it a target for the newly self-
     conscious Sinhalese majority.

241. Keeling, Desmond. "Central Training in the
     Civil Service: Some General Issues." *Public
     Administration* (London), 50 (Spring 1972),
     1-18.

     Follows earlier article, cited as item 242.
     Discusses what constitutes effective training
     courses and the problems involved in measuring
     the long-term impact of training. British in
     orientation.

242. Keeling, Desmond. "The Development of Central
     Training in the Civil Service, 1963-1970."
     Public Administration London), 49 (Spring
     1971), 51-71.

     Reviews the record of civil service training
     in Britain between the establishment of the
     Treasury Department's Centre for Administrative
     Studies in 1963 to the opening of the Civil
     Service College in 1970, pursuant to the
     recommendations of the Fulton Committee. Ar-
     gues that the most important changes that took
     place in this period were the institutional-
     ization of training in the Civil Service and
     the increased number of those receiving train-
     ing. See item 241.

243. Kellner, Peter and Lord Crowther-Hunt. *The
     Civil Servants: An Inquiry Into Britain's
     Ruling Class*. London and Sydney: Macdonald
     General Books, 1980.

     Investigation of the post-Fulton Civil
     Service in Britain by a member of the Fulton
     Committee (Crowther-Hunt) and a journalist
     (Kellner). The first section of the book
     outlines the Fulton recommendations and
     attempts to explain why they were never fully
     implemented. The second section describes
     contemporary recruitment practices for higher
     administrators. The third and concluding
     section focuses on several current problems
     in British administration, including secrecy
     and civil service-parliamentary relationships.

244. Kelly, Michael P. *White Collar Proletariat: The Industrial Behaviour of British Civil Servants.* London: Routledge and Kegan Paul, 1980.

    Empirical study of British civil servants as employees. Seeks to test the extent to which changes in the industrial behavior of civil servants are a product of "proletariani- zation," which is operationalized by reference to variables such as income, social origins, and work organization. Finds that increased militancy among white collar civil servants cannot be explained by reference to this con- cept.

245. Kernaghan, Kenneth. "Codes of Ethics and Public Administration: Progress, Problems, and Prospects." *Public Administration* (London), 58 (Summer 1980), 207-224.

    Examines the state of administrative ethics in Canada, with some reference to the U.S., Britain, and Australia. The 1970's witnessed a focus on written rules to combat unethical conduct, especially conflict of interest. Attempts have also been made to regulate post- employment activity, political activity, con- flicts of loyalties, and "leaks." The costs and benefits of formal codes of ethics are considered. Concludes by noting the importance of instilling an internal sense of administra- tive responsibility.

246. Kernaghan, Kenneth. "Representative Bureau- cracy: The Canadian Perspective." *Canadian Public Administration,* 21, 4 (Winter 1978), 489-512.

    After reviewing the theory of representative bureaucracy, describes Canadian government efforts to meet test of representativeness for francophones, women, and native people. Public policy in this area serves mainly sym- bolic and partisan political purposes. Pro- vides limited secondary data on representation of different groups.

247. Kim, Paul S. "Japan's National Civil Service
Commission: Its Origins and Structure."
Public Administration (London), 48 (Winter
1970), 405-421.

Begins with a discussion of the National
Public Service Law and the creation of the
National Personnel Authority (Civil Service
Commission), both of which had their roots
in the postwar occupation. Strains between
American and Japanese perceptions of civil
service structure and obligations noted. Concludes with an analysis of the 1965 reorganization of the Personnel Authority, which
altered the original concept of an independent
regulatory authority, and which is viewed as
a result of traditionalist attack.

248. Koh, B.C. "Stability and Change in Japan's
Higher Civil Service." *Comparative Politics*,
11, 3 (April 1979), 279-298.

Asks to what extent Japanese bureaucracy was
transformed in the desired direction by the
series of civil service reforms undertaken
after the Second World War. Concludes that
the Japanese bureaucracy has shown great
resilience and that while some change toward
greater openness has occurred, the persistence
of old patterns is striking.

249. Koslov, I.M. "The Relationship Between Colle-
gial and One-Man Management in Soviet State
Administration at the Present Stage of
Development." *Soviet Law and Government*,
3, 2 (Fall 1964), 3-12.

Soviet one-man management presupposes the
existence of collegiality and collective
leadership as rightfully embodying the principle of mass participation in the functioning
of state administrative apparatus.

250. Krislov, Samuel. *Representative Bureaucracy.*
      Englewood-Cliffs, New Jersey: Prentice-
      Hall, 1974.

      Begins with a reconsideration of the contro-
      versy over "representative bureaucracy"
      initiated by Kingsley: what does representative
      bureaucracy mean and what difference does it
      make? Explains the ways in which bureaucra-
      cies can and cannot be representative. Pre-
      sents case material on India, Malaya, Belgium,
      Canada, Lebanon, and Israel.

251. Kubota, Akira. *Higher Civil Servants in Post-
      war Japan.* Princeton: Princeton University
      Press, 1969.

      Examines the social origins, educational
      backgrounds, and bureaucratic and post-retire-
      ment careers of a sample of 1,353 people who
      held positions of section chief or above in
      the central Japanese bureaucracy. Social
      origins are heterogenous, though the educa-
      tional base was extremely narrow, with 80%
      of the elite coming from Tokyo Imperial Uni-
      versity. This educational homogeneity has
      produced great standardization of career
      patterns.

252. Kuklan, H. "Civil Service Reform in Iran:
      Myth and Reality." *International Review
      of Administrative Sciences,* 43, 4 (1977),
      345-351.

      After reviewing stages in evolution of
      Iranian Civil Service since 1922, argues
      against position classification system import-
      ed from U.S.

253. Kuruvilla, P.K. "The Career Concept in the
      Canadian Public Service." *International
      Review of Administrative Sciences,* 39, 1
      (1973), 49-55.

Addresses the question, to what extent
is the career concept present in the higher
Canadian Civil Service? Argues that traditional reliance on rank-in-job recruitment,
coupled with the use of appointments from
outside the service interfered with the career
notion. A new career assignment program has
been established to help ease these problems,
although more fundamental reforms will be
necessary before the career concept will be
fully achieved.

254. Laframboise, H.L. "Administrative Reform in
the Federal Public Service: Signs of a
Saturation Psychosis." *Canadian Public
Administration*, 14, 3 (Fall 1971), 303-325.

Managers in Canada's Civil Service have been
required in the last few years to introduce
and implement internal reforms that exceed
the absorptive capacity of the system, and
that have diverted them from their principal
duties. Singled out for criticism are the
Glassco Report recommendations, collective
bargaining and bilingualism. Suggests that
some of these reforms be reversed.

255. Leemans, Arne F. "Administrative Reform: An
Overview." *Development and Change*, 2, 2
(1970-1971), 1-18.

General discussion of the problem of
administrative reform, with emphasis on
developing countries. Essay introduces special
edition of journal on this subject, with five
companion pieces. Discusses objectives and
strategies of reform as well as problems of
theory-building.

256. Lewis, Paul H. "The Spanish Ministerial
Elite, 1938-1969." *Comparative Politics*,
5, 1 (October 1972), 83-106.

Studies the composition of the Council of
Ministers in the Franco era as a way of analyzing the extent to which authoritarian regimes
refresh themselves through turnover or allow
themselves to stagnate. Collected data on
age, birthplace, background, tenure, education,
and political affiliates of the 89 men who
occupied posts on the Council during this period.
Shows some adaptability, with tendency toward
a technical-bureaucratic elite.

257. Leys, Colin. "Administrative Training in
     Kenya." *Administrative Training and Develop-
     ment* (item 530).

     Discusses establishment of Kenya Institute
     of Administration in 1961 and traces its his-
     tory through 1969. Assesses strengths and
     weaknesses of Kenyan administrative training,
     and concludes that the KIA has kept alive key
     ideals of development despite conservative
     environmental pressures.

258. Lisitsyn, V. and G. Popov. "On Administrative
     Cadres." *The Soviet Review*, 10, 2 (Summer
     1969), 14-21.

     Technological advancement and the implementa-
     tion of a new system of planning and economic
     incentives necessitate revisions in managerial
     training. Closer attention to the science of
     management is needed to train economic command
     cadres.

259. Lompe, Klaus. "Scientific Counselling in
     Policy-Making in the Federal Republic of
     Germany." *International Review of Adminis-
     trative Sciences*, 35, 1 (1969), 1-10.

     Discusses problems of integrating scientists
     and scientific advisors--especially social
     scientists--into the German political-
     administrative system. Only recently has the
     gulf between politics and science in Germany
     begun to be bridged, with ministers, members

of parliament, and high administrators making greater use of social science information through various advisory groups.

260. Love, J.D. "Personnel Reorganization in the Canadian Public Service: Some Observations on the Past." *Canadian Public Administration*, 22, 3 (Autumn 1979), 402-414.

Reviews history of Canadian public personnel administration, with a focus on the Civil Service Act of 1918 and the Public Service Act of 1967. The former formally introduced the merit principle, while the latter allowed collective bargaining.

261. Lucas Tomés, José Luis. "Algumos Aspectos del Functionamiento de la Administración Pública." *International Review of Administrative Sciences*, 45, 3 (1979), 241-248.

Observations on the daily trials of central government administrators in Spain. Criticizes infeasibility of laws, personnel disruptions through frequent transfers, pointless reorganizations, poor classification practices, and lax supervision.

262. MacDonald, James and G.K. Fry. "Policy Planning Units--Ten Years On." *Public Administration* (London), 58 (Winter 1980), 421-438.

Although planning units have become integral parts of British central government, the kind of bright, young "in-and-outer" specialists admired by the Fulton Commission have not materialized. Article surveys 14 Departments, and finds that instead the policy planning systems developed in the 1970's extended and consolidated the normal patterns of British departmental administration. This is attributed to underlying socio-cultural norms.

263. Maheshwari, Shriram. "The All India Services." *Public Administration* (London), 49 (Autumn 1971), 291-308.

    The All India services--of which the Indian Administrative Service, the Indian Police Service, and the Indian Forest Service comprise the three most important--are personnel systems designed to allow free interchange of civil servants between central and state governments. Article reviews the creation and operation of these services, and concludes with a discussion of the arguments for and against their retention.

264. Mallaby, Sir George. "The Civil Service Commission: Its Place in the Machinery of Government." *Public Administration* (London), 42 (Spring 1964), 1-10.

    Member of the Civil Service Commission (CSC), which was a forerunner of the present British Civil Service Department, describes its objectives and relationships with the Treasury. Includes some statistical information on types and numbers of employees covered.

265. Mallet, Serge. *Bureaucracy and Technocracy in Socialist Countries*. Nottingham: Russell Peace Foundation, 1974.

    Brief Marxist analysis of the evolution and contemporary state of bureaucracy in Eastern Europe. Focuses on "technocratic-bureaucratic conflict." Argues that greater "social self-management" is needed to avoid bureaucratic excesses.

266. Marx, Fritz Morstein. "German Administration and the Speyer Academy." *Public Administration Review*, 27, 5 (December 1967), 403-410.

    Traces the history of the study of administration in Germany from 1727 (creation of

first chair in "cameral science"). Focuses
on the Speyer Academy, which opened in 1774.
Despite its long roots, administrative science
is somewhat an orphan in Germany, given the
strong emphasis on legal training for public
service.

267. Mathur, B.C. "Training of Civil Servants in
Japan." *Indian Journal of Public Administration*, 15, 2 (April/June 1969), 255-276.

Although formal institutional training is
comparatively new in Japan, the government is
now showing keen interest in developing training programs for all levels of officials.
Includes detailed tables outlining courses of
study for trainees.

* Mayntz, Renate and Fritz W. Scharpf. *Policy-
Making in the German Federal Republic*.
Cited as item 114.

268. Meier, Kenneth John. "Representative Bureaucracy: An Empirical Analysis." *American
Political Science Review*, 69, 2 (June 1975),
526-542.

Analytical critique of theories of representative bureaucracy, coupled with quantitative assessment of extent to which the U.S.
bureaucracy is representative. Includes comparisons between representativeness of American higher civil service with those of Britain,
France, Denmark, Turkey and India.

269. Meyers, François. "La Formation en Service des
Fonctionnaires Belges." *International Review of Administrative Sciences*, 45, 4
(1979), 321-330.

Discusses in-service training programs in
Belgium, which are presently conducted by
three organizations: the General Directorate
of Selection and Training, the Institute of

Administration, University, and the Standing
Committee for Promoting the Training of Public
Servants. While in general pleased with
progress of training, criticizes lack of
connection with career management.

270. Miller, Ernest G. "Management by Objectives
     in Great Britain." *Public Administration
     Review*, 30, 4 (July/August 1970), 436-437.

     Brief analysis of MBO status in Britain,
     largely derived from an article in the
     Economist. Suggests that MBO is receiving
     increasing attention, and that three films
     have recently been produced to disseminate
     the theory there.

271. Mills, Gladstone, et al. "The Attitudes and
     Behavior of the Senior Civil Service in
     Jamaica." *Social and Economic Studies*,
     23, 2 (June 1974), 311-363.

     Jamaican civil servants see themselves
     entirely as implementors, not as policy formu-
     lators. They lack commitment and ideological
     strength. This is typical of the Caribbean
     "bureaucratic malaise." Attitudinal data
     presented based on survey of 100 top officials.

272. Minogue, Martin. "The Public Administration
     in Mauritius." *Journal of Administration
     Overseas*, 15, 3 (July 1976), 160-166.

     Presents brief overview of the historical
     development of the Mauritian public services
     and of current problems in Mauritian public
     administration. Administrative machinery is
     inadequate, and reform is urgently needed.

273. Molitor, André. *L'Administration de la
     Belgique*. Bruxelles: Centre de Recherche
     et d'Information, 1974.

General overview of Belgian public administration. Provides history of public service,
the relationship between politics and administration, and a summary of administrative law
questions. Offers detailed analysis of
departmental organization, personnel systems,
and budgetary processes.

274. Moor, P. "L'Organisation de l'Administration
Federale de la Confederation Suisse."
*International Review of Administrative
Sciences,* 45, 3 (1979), 207-213.

Discusses the Federal Council and Federal
Administration Act of 1978 which was designed
to smooth interdepartmental coordination. The
results have been "unspectacular," for the Act
did little other than to add staff. No basic
change in structural relations was forthcoming,
owing to Swiss federalism.

275. Moreux, Gilbert. "Ambiguous Unionism."
International Journal of Politics, 2, 2-3
(Summer/Fall 1972), 147-162.

Considers French civil service unionism
against the backdrop of the May 1968 protests.
Criticizes their conservatism and self-
protective impulses. Examines in particular
the operations of unions within the Finance
Ministry.

276. Nakib, Khalil and Monte Palmer. Traditional-
ism and Change Among Lebanese Bureaucrats."
*International Review of Administrative
Sciences,* 42, 1 (1976), 15-22.

Based on interviews with 162 Lebanese civil
servants conducted in 1972, concludes that
despite an apparently more modern context,
Lebanese bureaucrats remain particularistic
and family oriented, in line with other middle
Eastern countries. Moreover, higher levels
of education do not produce a greater propen-
sity for bureaucratic change.

277. Nolting, Orin. *Post-Entry Training in the Public Service in Western Europe*. Chicago: International City Managers Association, 1972.

    Focuses on post-recruitment training of public administrators at the municipal level in Austria, Belgium, Denmark, England, Finland, France, Germany, Ireland, Italy, Luxembourg, Netherlands, Norway, Spain, Sweden, Switzerland, and Yugoslavia. Consists of short, narrative descriptions of procedures for each country.

278. Osman, Osama A. "Formalism v. Realism: The Saudi Arabian Experience with Position Classification." *Public Personnel Management*, 7, 3 (May/June 1978), 177-181.

    Discusses implementation of position classification in Saudi public personnel system. Argues that Saudis have modified system to some extent to adapt to local conditions.

279. Osman, Osama A. "Saudi Arabia: An Unprecedented Growth of Wealth with an Unparalleled Growth of Bureaucracy." *International Review of Administrative Sciences*, 45, 3 (1979), 234-240.

    Overview of administrative problems of Saudi Arabia. Although Saudi Arabia, unlike other developing countries, does not lack capital, it does face common problems of poor bureaucratic performance and overstaffing. Includes organization tables, and some budget and personnel data.

280. Painter, C. "The Civil Service: Post-Fulton Malaise." *Public Administration* (London), 53 (Winter 1975), 427-442.

    Argues that Fulton's overconcern with structural questions, and corollary inattention to questions of motivation and human

relations, have led to widespread staff dis-
content in the aftermath of the reforms.
Many of the remarks in the article are directed to the 1975 report of the Wider Issues
Review Team, issued as *Civil Servants and
Change,* a British Government study which
identified these problems.

281. Papastathopoulos, C.D. "Civil Service Reforms
in Greece: 1950-1964." *International Review
of Administrative Sciences,* 30, 4 (1964),
373-384.

In 1951, the Greek Parliament enacted a
revised Civil Service Code which provides the
basis for the Greek public service. Its provisions are outlined and analyzed in detail
here, as are problems that have arisen since
its enactment. Suggests strengthening the
central personnel agency, reducing Parliamentary involvement in the civil service, reducing the number of temporary employees,
revising the salary structure and reorganizing
the government.

282. Parris, H. "Twenty Years of l'Ecole National
d'Administration." *Public Administration*
(London), 43 (Winter 1965), 395-411.

Descriptive treatment of ENA. Outlines
entrance requirements, course subjects, and
background of candidates, with supplementary
statistics. Concludes with lessons for Britain's administrative training.

283. Pastori, G. "L'Administration du Personnel
et la Bureaucratie." *International Review
of Administrative Sciences,* 37, 1-2 (1971),
52-58.

Critically examines personnel practices
in Italian central government. Finds basic
system installed in 1957 to be outdated. Full
uniformity has not been achieved in classification, and little control exists; yet the

system is without flexibility. Notes 1968 and
1970 reforms designed to reinvigorate system,
including the establishment of an ENA-like
school.

284. Pinto-Duschinsky, Michael. "Corruption in
Britain." *Political Studies*, 25, 2 (June
1977), 274-284.

Examines the extent of corruption in British
public service in the wake of the report of
the (1974-76) Royal Commission, which the
author believes underestimated the problem.
Briefly reviews American state crime commissions, and argues for a permanent anti-
corruption agency in Britain.

285. Presthus, Robert. "Mrs. Thatcher Stalks
the Quango: A Note on Patronage and Justice
in Britain." *Public Administration Review*,
41, 3 (May/June 1981), 312-317.

Cutting the number and growth of quasi-
public agencies (quangos), which now total
some 30,000, is a major element in the
Thatcher Government's economic program.
Quangos are generally designed to serve
interest-representation and advisory functions
to the permanent bureaucracy. To date, the
Prime Minister's efforts have produced little
retrenchment, although the symbolism of her
activities is seen as important.

286. Pross, A. Paul and V. Seymour Wilson.
"Graduate Education in Canadian Public
Administration: Antecedents, Present Trends
and Portents." *Canadian Public Administration*, 19, 4 (Winter 1976), 515-541.

Reviews changes in Canadian public administration graduate education, with focus on
recent revival. Discusses intellectual origins
of field in Canada, and relationship to political science and political economy. The
institutionalization of the separation of
public administration from political science

will ultimately strengthen both disciplines.

287. Raphaeli, Nimrod. "The Absorption of
      Orientals into Israeli Bureaucracy."
      Middle Eastern Studies, 8, 1 (January 1972),
      85-92.

      Begins by noting large immigration to Israel
      from East Europe, Middle East, and North
      Africa, and asks how effectively people from
      these regions have been absorbed into the
      Israeli bureaucracy. Provides background
      information on Israeli Civil Service, and
      aggregate data on Service characteristics,
      including distribution of officials by birth-
      place, education, and year of immigration.
      Concludes that while overall representation
      of Orientals is good, there is a skewing by
      level of position such that these people
      occupy a disproportionate number of low level
      jobs.

288. Raphaeli, Nimrod. "The Senior Civil Service
      in Israel: Notes on Some Characteristics."
      Public Administration (London), 48, (Summer
      1970), 169-178.

      Describes structure of Israeli Civil Ser-
      vice, with focus on senior grade administra-
      tors. Includes eight tables presenting data
      on age, occupation, birthplace, education,
      length of service, etc. Notes on overall
      professionalization and upgrading of the
      senior civil service in recent years, although
      continuing efforts at depoliticization are
      needed.

289. Rendel, Margherita. *The Administrative
      Functions of the Conseil D'Etat.* London:
      Weidenfeld and Nicolson, 1970.

      Detailed descriptive analysis of the
      origins, structure and functions of the French
      Conseil d'Etat. Discusses recruitment and

career paths of members, organization of work and relationships with other public officials.

290. Reñón, Alberto G. "The Spanish Public Service." *International Review of Administrative Sciences*, 35, 2-3 (1969), 133-140.

Overview of the Spanish civil service. Detailed description of recruitment, career principles, classification system, terms of employment, remuneration and retirement. Includes some statistics on numbers of employees and pay scales.

291. Rich, H. "Higher Civil Servants in Ontario, Canada: An Administrative Elite in Comparative Perspective." *International Review of Administrative Sciences*, 41, 1 (1975), 67-74.

Provides data on the class background of senior civil servants in Ontario. Finds over-representation of higher status groups. Concludes with a consideration of the significance of elite background analyses, and casts doubt on the import of social origin.

292. Richards, Peter G. *Patronage in British Government*. London: George Allen and Unwin, Ltd., 1963.

General historical and contemporary analysis of British patronage. Following introductory material on the meaning and implications of patronage, provides focused treatment of patronage in the civil service, on administrative boards and advisory bodies, in judicial tribunals, and in the church and peerage.

293. Rimlinger, Gaston V. "Administrative Training and Modernisation in Zaire." *Journal of Development Studies*, 12, 4 (July 1976), 364-382.

Analyzes the rise and fall of the Ecole
Nationale d'Administration (ENDA) of Kinshasa
from 1961-1971. This experience parallels
that of public administration training
institutes in other developing countries.
Common themes include search for role and
status, conflict with academic establishments,
and difficult relationships with technical
assistance agencies.

294. Rizos, E. John. "Public Administration in
Greece: The Quest for 1981." *International
Review of Administrative Sciences*, 46, 4
(1980), 327-332.

Brief overview of the state of public
administration in Greece on eve of entry into
EEC. Lists five elements of Greek bureaucratic culture that inhibit its effectiveness,
with suggestions for change.

295. Robson, William A. "The Fulton Report on the
Civil Service." *Political Quarterly*, 39, 4
(October/December 1968), 397-414.

Attacks Fulton Report for succumbing to the
hysteria of public opinion, which was looking
for a scapegoat for British problems and
found it in the Civil Service. Defends idea
of generalist, which is distinguished from
amateur. Too little evidence is offered for
any of the conclusions of the Fulton Report.

*   Roos, Leslie L. Jr. and Noralou P. Roos.
"Administrative Change in a Modernizing
Society." Cited as 132.

296. Rosenbloom, David H. and David Nachmias.
"Bureaucratic Representation in Israel."
Public Personnel Management, 3, 4 (July/
August 1974), 303-313.

After a general overview of the representative bureaucracy literature, applies concept

in Israeli case. Based on sample of 1,602
civil servants. Focuses on seniority, education, age, place of birth and year of immigra-
tion. Finds that passive underrepresentation
and unequal distribution are not necessarily
linked to discriminatory practices.

297. Roy, Delwin A. "Management Education and
      Training in the Arab World." *International
      Review of Administrative Sciences*, 43, 3
      (1977), 221-228.

      Although most Arab countries have establish-
      ed organizations to train public employees,
      there is a need to develop bodies of expert
      knowledge more directly relevant to Arab
      developmental problems rather than rely on
      Western experience.

298. Roy, W.T. "The Influence of the Chinese
      Examination System on British Imperial
      Administration." *New Zealand Journal of
      Public Administration*, 35, 2 (March 1973),
      49-59.

      Assesses the degree to which the adoption
      of competitive examinations for bureaucratic
      recruitment by the British colonial service
      represents a deliberate imitation of the
      Chinese model. Considers alternative hypothe-
      ses. Ultimately concludes that while the
      Chinese model had some influence, the British
      adopted a similar system because they faced
      the same problems administering a vast empire
      as did the Chinese mandarinate.

299. Ruiz de Elvira, José María and Alberto
      Gutierrez Reñon. "La Figura del Administra-
      dor General y su Reclutamiento en la
      Administración Pública Española."
      *International Review of Administrative
      Sciences*, 31, 3 (1965), 227-232.

      The Spanish Civil Service Act of 1963 was

promulgated in part to provide Spain with a
cadre of top civil servants comparable to
Britain's administrative class and the French
administrateurs civils. Prior to this,
officials were splintered into some 250
different groups (cuerpos) of specialists.
This led to compartmentalization and an
inability to adapt to change.

300. Ryavec, Karl W. "Soviet Industrial Manage-
     ment, 1965-70." *Canadian Slavic Studies*,
     5, 2 (Summer 1971), 151-177.

     Discusses problems of Soviet management in
     the context of political and economic changes
     in the environment. The successful manage-
     ment of military production has not been
     transferred to the non-military sector, in
     part because these problems have not been
     assigned as high a priority by political
     leaders. Managers do not innovate because of
     a lack of incentives and autonomy. True
     managerial reform will require restructuring
     relationships between the Party, ministries
     and functional experts.

301. Sala Arquer, José Manuel. "La Noción Juridica
     de Servicio Publico." *International Review
     of Administrative Sciences*, 42, 3 (1976),
     266-270.

     Contrary to interpretations of some scholars,
     the notion of public service in Spain arose
     independent of French influence. At least
     since the mid-19th century, a distinctly
     Spanish body of administrative law can be dis-
     cerned.

302. Schmidt, Folke. "Collective Negotiations
     Between the State and its Officials."
     *International Review of Administrative
     Sciences*, 28, 3 (1962), 298-305.

     Comparative analysis of public sector labor

law in Great Britain, Germany, France and
Sweden. Discusses various categories of
workers and their rights with respect to
collective bargaining. Brief examination of
right-to-strike issue.

303. Schwartz, Charles A. "Corruption and Political Development in the U.S.S.R." *Comparative Politics*, 11, 4 (July 1979), 425-444.

Analyzes extent and functions of Soviet
administrative corruption, using Soviet news-
paper accounts for data. Discusses report pad-
ding, embezzlement, abuse of authority and
bribery.

304. Sepe, Onorato. "Les Différenciations dans le
Traitement des Fonctionnaires on Italie."
*International Review of Administrative
Sciences*, 45, 2 (1979), 156-164.

Discusses pay inequalities in Italy. Stan-
dard salary scales are misleading, for salaries
are often supplemented by a welter of allow-
ances and bonuses due to lack of sound personnel practices, union pressures and general
laxity.

305. Sheriff, Peta F. "Outsiders in a Closed
Career: The Example of the British Civil
Service." *Public Administration* (London),
50 (Winter 1972), 397-417.

Examines the effects on morale and performance in the British Civil Service of
recruitment of "outside" administrators, those
who do not follow the normal closed career
pattern. Data drawn from biographical analysis and interviews with direct entry princi-
pals. Finds that "open" recruitment has
broadened the experiential base of the Service,
although effects have been limited. Any great
expansion of system, however, would damage
morale.

306. Siegel, Gilbert. "The Strategy of Public
     Administration Reform: The Case of Brazil."
     Public Administration Review, 26, 1 (March
     1966), 45-55.

     Notes that while American administrative
     theory has long counseled centralization of
     budgeting, purchasing, and personnel prac-
     tices to achieve economy and efficiency, this
     approach is not universally applicable. Study
     of the Brazilian Administrative Department
     of the Public Service (DASP) suggests need
     for "empirical approach" to administrative
     reform.

307. Siegel, Gilbert and K. Nascimento. "Formalism
     in Brazilian Administrative Reform."
     International Review of Administrative
     Sciences, 31, 3 (1965), 175-184.

     Case study of the installation of position
     classification in the Brazilian federal govern-
     ment as a way of explaining the prevalence of
     administrative formalism. The main causes of
     formalism are resistance from power centers to
     changes in the status quo and technical diffi-
     culties in carrying out reform.

308. Silberman, Bernard S. "Traditional Values
     or Organizational Imperatives in the
     Japanese Upper Civil Service." Journal of
     Asian Studies, 32, 2 (February 1973), 251-
     264.

     Describes "ringisei" system of bureaucratic
     decision-making in post-Meiji Japan (1968-
     1945). This is a system of decision-making
     from "below," where lower-level specialists
     act first, circulating documents for approval
     horizontally and vertically in the administra-
     tive hierarchy. Argues that this is a
     response to high rates of mobility.

309. Singhi, Marendra K. "Job Satisfaction Among
     Bureaucrats in an Indian State." *Philip-
     pine Journal of Public Administration,* 37,
     2 (April 1973), 227-241.

     Examines five aspects of job satisfaction
     (nature of work, power, prestige, and promo-
     tion chances) among 575 public and private-
     sector bureaucrats in India. Finds widely
     varying orientations. Strong relationship
     found between position in hierarchy and satis-
     faction, which is interpreted as a reflection
     of status gaps left from colonial and feudal
     periods.

310. Sisson, Charles H. *The Spirit of British
     Administration.* London: Faber, 1966.

     Analysis presented as an aggregate "character
     study" of British civil service. Extensive
     comparisons drawn with Germany, France, Sweden,
     and Spain. Overall, a favorable picture pre-
     sented, with a clear appreciation of tradi-
     tional British empiricism and pragmatism.

311. Smith, Brian G. "Reform and Change in British
     Central Administration." *Political Studies,*
     19, 2 (June 1971), 213-226.

     Distinguishes between administrative reform
     (political) and administrative change (organi-
     zational). The former has a moral content,
     the latter does not. Illustrated by a dis-
     cussion of the Northcote-Trevelyan and Fulton
     reforms.

312. Smith, Theodore. "Stimulating Performance
     in the Indonesian Bureaucracy: Gaps in the
     Administrator's Tool Kit." *Educational
     Development and Cultural Change,* 23, 4
     (July 1975), 719-738.

     Reviews strategies to increase bureaucratic
     productivity in Indonesia through the appli-

cation of personnel incentives and sanctions.
Suggests that peculiar historical, cultural
and political factors have hitherto limited
the application of sound personnel techniques.
More attention should be paid to salaries,
salary supplements, promotion and other
incentives. Includes data on pay and performance in Indonesia.

313. Smith, Thomas. *The New Zealand Bureaucrat*.
      New Zealie: Cheshire, 1974.

      Empirical study of midlevel New Zealand
      bureaucrats. Based on interviews with 119
      officials. Analyzes career patterns, duties,
      role expectations, job satisfaction, superior-
      subordinate relations, political pressures,
      and the role of women.

314. Somerhausen, Marc. "L'Evolution du Droit
      Administratif Belge." *International Review
      of Administrative Sciences*, 45, 4 (1979),
      298-306.

      Growth and structure of the Belgian Civil
      Service described, with an emphasis on
      administrative law and conditions of employ-
      ment.

315. Spaulding, Robert M. Jr. *Imperial Japan's
      Higher Civil Service Examinations*. Prince-
      ton: Princeton University Press, 1967.

      Historical analysis of the evolution and
      operation of "the key to the Japanese bureau-
      cracy," the civil service examination system.
      Put in overall context of Japanese moderniza-
      tion from 1869 to 1945. Contrast drawn with
      China, which abolished its merit system under
      pressures of modernization. Argues that there
      was a direct connection between the rigor and
      impersonality of the examination system and
      the effectiveness of the Japanese bureaucracy.
      They also contributed indirectly to the ero-
      sion of feudalism in Japanese society.

Includes detailed appendices, with examination questions presented.

316. Stack, Freida. "Civil Service Associations and the Whitley Report of 1917." *Political Quarterly*, 40, 3 (July/September 1969), 283-295.

   Reviews history of British civil service labor relations up to issuance of the Whitley Report, which established a system, still in existence, of joint consultation. Concludes with a brief review of the fifty years of Whitley Council operation.

*   Stahl, O.G. "Managerial Effectiveness in Developing Countries." Cited as item 542.

*   Stamp, Patricia. "The East African Staff College." Cited as item 543.

317. Stenning, Ron. "Contemporary Trends in Labour Relations in the United Kingdom's Public Sector." *Personnel Management*, 9, 4 (July/August 1980), 302-311.

   Discusses reforms in British labor relations. Argues that some reforms have been overtaken by changes in the political and economic environment and by growing judicial interventions.

318. Stevens, Anne. "The Role of the Ecole Nationale d'Administration." *Public Administration* (London), 56 (Autumn 1978), 283-298.

   Reviews the creation and operation of ENA. Presents a functionalist analysis of its role in the French civil service. Argues that even though it has not accomplished many of its major formal objectives, it serves to reinforce certain historical traditions, and is thus valued in the French administrative system.

319. Stuttmeier, Richard P. "The Gikan Question in Japanese Government: Bureaucratic Curiosity or Institutional Failure?" *Asian Survey*, 13, 20 (October 1978), 1046-1066.

Discusses specialist-generalist problem in Japanese bureaucracy. Gikan is the term given to technical officials. Data on numbers of gikan by ministry, salary levels, and rates of promotion presented. Generalist bias predominates.

320. Subramaniam, V. "The Relative Status of Specialists and Generalists: An Attempt at a Comparative Historical Explanation." *Public Administration* (London), 46 (Autumn 1968), 331-340.

Analyzes why Britain is "odd man out" in poor integration of specialists into Civil Service. Argues that roots lie in "gentleman amateur" image of proper administrator. Comparisons drawn with U.S., Australia, India, Pakistan, Ceylon, Canada, and Ireland.

321. Suleiman, Ezra N. "The Myth of Technical Expertise: Selection, Organization, and Leadership." *Comparative Politics*, 10, 1 (October 1977), 137-158.

Challenges the idea that technical specialization is the foundation of power for elite administrators in France. ENA training may be specialized but it has little impact on the diverse posts its graduates will occupy. The administrators themselves believe that their generalist skills are far more important.

322. Thrash, Robert M. "Establishing a Merit
     System in Ecuador: A Progress Report."
     Public Personnel Review, 27, 2 (April 1966),
     122-124.

     Reviews forty years of civil service reform
     in Ecuador, beginning with the draft merit
     law of 1924. Progress began to be made in
     the early 1960's with the counsel of the U.S.
     AID mission. Now Ecuador has become an "out-
     standing" example of the possibilities of
     merit personnel systems in developing nations.

*   Tice, Robert D. "Administrative Structure,
     Ethnicity, and Nation-Building in the Ivory
     Coast." Cited as item 139.

323. Tickner, P.J. "Ethical Guidelines for
     Administrators." *Public Administration
     Review*, 34, 6 (November/December 1974),
     587-592.

     Discusses the basic "rules of the game"
     in the British civil service, as they define
     ethical conduct. Begins with an examination
     of the doctrine of ministerial responsibility,
     treats the idea of collegial decision-making,
     and norms about secrecy and personal integrity.
     Concludes with the observation that actual
     examples of corruption and unethical behavior
     in Britain are very low, and those that are
     identified are dealt with harshly.

324. Tsien, T. "Evolution de la Conception du
     Fonctionnaire en Chine." *International
     Review of Administrative Sciences*, 38, 4
     (1972), 385-392.

     A capsule history of Chinese civil service
     from earliest times through the cultural
     revolution. Some discussion of the current
     problem of balancing ideological purity with
     administrative competence.

325. Tsien, T. "Organisation et Structure Adminis-
     tratives en Republique Populaire du Chine."
     *International Review of Administrative
     Sciences*, 43, 4 (1977), 309-320.

     Reviews basic principles of Chinese adminis-
     tration and democratic centralism, double
     subordination, collegiality and the "triple
     union."

326. Vaison, Robert A. "Collective Bargaining in
     the Federal Public Service: The Achievement
     of a Milestone in Personnel Relations."
     Canadian Public Administration, 12, 1
     (Spring 1969), 108-122.

     Historical perspective on collective negotia-
     tions in Canadian public sector, culminating
     in analysis of the Public Staff Relations Act
     of 1967. This piece of legislation provided
     for truly bilateral negotiations for the first
     time.

327. Verner, Joel G. "Characteristics of Adminis-
     trative Personnel: The Case of Guatemala."
     Journal of Developing Areas, 5, 1 (October
     1970), 73-86.

     Examines backgrounds of a stratified sample
     of high Guatemalan public officials in an
     effort to assess quality of administrative
     service. Concentrates on following character-
     istics: sex, age, residence, experience, role
     perceptions, pre-entry occupation, recruitment
     route, education, training, and motivation.
     Presents data in tabular form and provides
     composite picture of the average elite Guate-
     malan civil servant.

328. Villanueva, Florencia C. "Performance Rating
     and Promotion: The DBP Experience."
     Philippine Journal of Public Administration,
     9, 4 (October 1975), 315-327.

Empirical study of the relationships between
performance ratings and promotion. Data from
personnel records of the Philippine Development Bank. Finds no relationship between
ratings and promotion.

329. Vogel, Lorentz. "La Réforme de la Procédure
Administration Suédoise." *International
Review of Administrative Sciences,* 40, 3
(1974), 207-215.

Reviews four procedural reforms in Swedish
administrative law undertaken in 1971: (1)
reorganization of the Supreme Administrative
Court workload; (2) establishment of County
Administrative Courts; (3) simplification and
codification of rules of procedure; and (4)
new rules governing agency decisional processes.

330. Weaver, Jerry L. "Value Patterns of a Latin
American Bureaucracy." *Human Relations,*
23, 3 (June 1970), 225-233.

Examines Guatemalan bureaucrats' values
toward public service. Data drawn from random
sample of 250 bureaucrats in 23 administrative
agencies. Finds high value placed on continued
employment, low values attached to reform,
innovation and risk-taking.

331. Williams, Richard, James Walker and Olive
Fletcher. "International Review of Staff
Appraisal Practices: Current Trends and
Issues." *Public Personnel Management,* 6, 1
(January/February 1977), 5-12.

Discusses personnel appraisal practices in
ten countries. Identifies several major
trends, including greater openness in appraisal expanded employee participation, and
increased legislative intervention. Argues
that most appraisal schemes are inadequately
monitored by organizations.

332. Wilson, A. Jeyaratnam. "The Public Service
     Commission and Ministerial Responsibility:
     The Ceylonese Experience." *Public Adminis-*
     tration (London), 40 (Spring 1968), 81-93.

     Descriptive treatment of Ceylonese Civil
     Service, and its governing body, the Public
     Service Commission (PSC). Discusses the
     PSC's powers and functions, its relationships
     with politicians, and the extent of its dele-
     gation of power.

333. Wright, Maurice. "The Professional Conduct
     of Civil Servants." *Public Administration*
     (London), 51 (Spring 1973), 1-16.

     Analyzes the ethical norms that guide the
     conduct of the British civil servant. Criti-
     cizes the Fulton Report for inattention to
     the issue, and notes considerable confusion
     over standards of professional conduct. Sug-
     gests that change is occurring in the direction
     of articulating previously unstated principles
     of conduct.

334. Ybema, S.B. and J. Wessel. "Le Mecanisme de
     Recours Contre les Actes Administratifs aux
     Pay-Bas." *International Review of Adminis-*
     trative Sciences, 39, 1 (1973), 1-13.

     Describes processes of judicial review of
     administrative action in the Netherlands by
     ordinary courts and administrative tribunals.
     Also treats appeals procedures within agencies.
     Recommends a consolidation of the review
     machinery to reduce its complexity.

*   Ziring, Lawrence and Robert LaPorte, Jr. "The
     Pakistan Bureaucracy: Two Views." Cited as
     item 553.

CHAPTER 6

ORGANIZATIONAL THEORY AND BEHAVIOR

Organization theory deals primarily with the
motivations, dispositions, and behaviors of men
and women at work. It seeks to explain how and
why people act as they do in complex organizations.
Although the distinction between organization
theory and personnel administration (the subject of
the previous chapter) is a troublesome one, it is
perhaps accurate to say that personnel administration is applied organization theory. Some central
questions for organization theory, as found in the
references offered in this chapter, are: What are
the sources of innovation in organization? Why do
bureaucratic routines develop? How do organizations respond to changes in the environment?

335. Bakvis, Herman. "French Canada and the
     'Bureaucratic Phenomenon'." *Canadian Public
     Administration*, 21, 1 (Spring 1978), 103-
     124.

     Attempts to identify unique French-Canadian
     characteristics and to assess their impact on
     administrative behavior. Uses Crozier's (item
     346) framework, with particular attention to
     authority relationships. Partially confirms
     Crozier's hypotheses. French Canadians have
     a more absolutist view of authority than
     English Canadians, in part owing to Catholic
     tradition. This does not necessarily lead to
     avoidance of face-to-face relations, however.

336. Beck, Carl. "Bureaucratic Conservatism and
     Innovation in Eastern Europe." *Comparative*

Political Studies, 1, 2 (July 1968), 275-
294.

Major hypothesis is that the role of the
state bureaucracy in the process of innovation
in Eastern Europe is partly a product of other
"structural and behavioral relationships" in
politics. The innovative role of bureaucracy
will increase when increased participation
makes uncontrolled system-wide innovations
stimulated by outside groups too costly.

337. Bent, Frederick. "The Turkish Bureaucracy as
      as Agent of Change." Journal of Comparative
      Administration, 1, 1 (May 1969), 47-64.

      Reports results of a 1966 survey of 336
      Turkish bureaucrats in seven central govern-
      ment ministries. Designed to provide data
      on social backgrounds, attitudes toward work,
      values placed on initiative, and status and
      prestige of public service. Finds urban cul-
      ture somewhat more supportive of change than
      is generally acknowledged, though recognizes
      inhibiting qualities of administrative sub-
      culture.

338. Bhattacharya, Mohit. "Bureaucratic Response
      to Emergency: An Empirical Study." Indian
      Journal of Public Administration, 20, 4
      (October/December 1974), 846-867.

      Presents findings of field studies in two
      districts of Maharashtra, which was struck by
      drought and famine conditions in 1971 and
      1973. Attempts to explain nature of adminis-
      trative organization developed to meet the
      emergency. Found that organizational structure
      was much less rigid and inflexible than usual.

339. Bonifacio, Manuel F. "Self-Discipline and
      Organization Behavior." Philippine Journal
      of Public Administration, 17, 1 (January
      1973), 58-67.

Anthropological analysis of Filipino organizations. Argues that formal organizational behavior reflects socialization to extended family ties and personalistic relationships. Filipino organizations adapt to this social style rather than to the norms of Western bureaucracy.

340. Bosetzky, Horst. "Forms of Bureaucratic Organization in Public and Industrial Administrations." *International Studies of Management and Organization*, 10, 4 (Winter 1980-81), 58-73.

Notes isomorphism between society and organizations on the dimension of bureaucratization in the German Federal Republic. Contrasts public and private organizations, noting forces that lead to variable debureaucratization and bureaucratization. Bureaucracy is decreasing in state administration and increasing in the private sector, even though overall levels are higher in the former.

341. Bowden, Peter. "Structure and Creativity: A Civil Service Hypothesis." *Public Administration* (London), 57 (Autumn 1979), 287-308.

Evaluates the adaptive capacity of the British Civil Service in the context of theories of innovation. Many of the factors said to inhibit innovation are present in the British administrative organization and are responsible for its inability to change and respond to new challenges. Suggests the enlargement and institutionalization of ministerial staff as remedy.

342. Brown, R.G.S. *The Administrative Process in Britain*. London: Methuen and Co., 1970.

Attempts to apply the insights of modern organization theory to administrative problems in British central government. Argues

that existing analyses tend either to rely on
"common sense" approaches to management or to
articulate a clear understanding of the role
of public administration in the political
process. Book divided into three parts: (1)
brief review of the development of the British
Civil Service through the Fulton Report; (2)
an introduction to organization theory; and
(3) an application or organization theory to
problems of management, recruitment, and planning. One of the major conclusions is the
Fulton recommendation to jettison the generalist administrator is misguided.

*   Brugger, William. *Democracy and Organization
        in the Chinese Industrial Enterprise.* Cited
        as item 174.

343.   Caiden, Gerald. "Coping with Turbulence:
        Israel's Administrative Experience."
        Journal of Comparative Administration, 1, 3
        (November 1969), 259-280.

        Examines Israeli administrative responses
        to environmental change. Focuses on Labour
        Zionist pioneers who have defined the
        administrative subculture. Demonstrated
        strong adaptive capabilities to deal with
        constant crises and uncertainty.

344.   Chackerian, Richard. "A Russian's View of
        Organizational Theory." *Public Administra-
        tion Review,* 36, 2 (March/April 1976), 202-
        203.

        Brief review of D. Gvishiani's Organizations
        and Management. Provides insight into con-
        temporary Soviet views of organizational
        processes. Notes Gvishiani's positive apprais-
        als of the classic management theories (Tay-
        lor, Gulick and Urwick, etc), and the mixed
        assessment of the human relations approach.

345. Constas, Helen. "The U.S.S.R.--From Charis-
     matic Sect to Bureaucratic Society."
     Administrative Science Quarterly, 6, 3
     (December 1961), 282-298.

     Argues that Soviet administration is best
     characterized as "charismatic bureaucracy"
     rather than legal-rational, as in West.
     Parallels are noted with Incan Peru and
     Pharaonic Egypt. The main purpose of such a
     bureaucracy is to extend state power and
     guarantee charismatic claims to superiority.

346. Crozier, Michel. *The Bureaucratic Phenomenon.*
     Chicago: The University of Chicago Press,
     1964.

     Explains the development of bureaucratic
     routines and the persistence of dysfunctional
     "vicious cycles" of behavior within organiza-
     tions by reference to a theory of power rela-
     tions in bureaucracy. Argues for cultural
     theories of organization. Presents case
     studies of two French bureaucracies--a cleri-
     cal agency and an industrial monopoly--to
     illustrate arguments.

347. Crozier, Michel. "Indications of Change in
     the Pattern of French Administration."
     Human Relations, 19, 3 (August 1966), 323-
     325.

     Elaboration of some themes from *The Bureau-
     cratic Phenomenon* (item 346). Reviews basic
     characteristics of French organizational
     patterns. Argues that "crisis" traditionally
     has been the distinctive style of French
     collective action. This pattern has become
     costly and inefficient, however. Maintains
     that new styles of collective action now
     appearing, especially among peasantry. New
     emphasis on interpersonal dialogue and commu-
     nication.

348. Crozier, Michel and Jean-Claude Thoenig. "The
     Regulation of Complex Organizational Sys-
     tems." *Administrative Science Quarterly*,
     21, 4 (December 1976), 547-570.

     Organizational analysis of French local
     government. Reports research in three
     departments: Some, Allier, and Herault, where
     527 officials were interviewed. Argues that
     collective decisions are managed by a complex
     but stable and organized system of institu-
     tions and groups. Stresses concepts of power,
     interorganizational networks, bargaining, and
     rules of the game.

349. Daland, Robert T. "Attitudes Toward Change
     Among Brazilian Bureaucrats." *Journal of
     Comparative Administration*, 4, 2 (August
     1972), 167-204.

     Reports on dispositions toward change among
     elite administrators in Brazil. Based on
     interviews with 325 officials. Especially
     interested in how traditional civilian bureau-
     crats have adapted to reform goals of Brazilian
     military regime. Concludes that a technocrat-
     ic alliance has arisen between civilian and
     military elites. These two groups share basic
     attitudes toward business of government.

350. Diamant, Alfred. "Tradition and Innovation in
     French Administration." *Comparative Politi-
     cal Studies*, 1, 2 (July 1968), 252-274.

     Addresses some central questions of innova-
     tion in French administration in the context
     of two case studies, one on regional adminis-
     tration and economic planning, the other of
     personnel in the higher service. Suggests that
     the administrative elite themselves are the
     main source of innovation, though they are
     unlikely to take actions (as in personnel
     policy) that would dilute their power or
     diminish their prestige. It is clear that
     far-reaching innovation needs support from

politicians, and not just civil servants, however.

*   Dresang, Dennis. "Entrepreneuralism and
    Development Administration." Cited as item
    482.

351. El-Namaki, M.S.S. "The Effectiveness and the
Managerial Behaviour of Company Boards in
Tanzania." *International Review of
Administrative Sciences,* 42, 3 (1976), 241-
247.

Analyzes the structure and behavior of
boards of directors of Tanzanian parastatal
organizations. Among the weaknesses identified are: nonprofessional orientations among
members, lack of product expertise, and ab-
sence of material incentives for board members. Suggests several reforms designed to
enhance the effectiveness of the boards,
including selection of specialists as members
and the allocation to them of specific functional responsibilities.

352. El-Namaki, M.S.S. "Matrix Organization: A
Possible Solution to the Organizational
Problems of the Tanzanian Export Sector?"
*International Review of Administrative
Sciences,* 44, 3 (1978), 277-282.

Argues that the use of matrix organizations
may alleviate many of the problems obstruct-
ing the flow of Tanzanian exports to overseas
markets.

353. Fallers, Lloyd. *Bantu Bureaucracy.* Chicago:
The University of Chicago Press, 1965.

Social-anthropological study of institutional change among the people of Busogo, a
province of Eastern Uganda. Describes the
traditional state system, as well as colonial

and transitional periods. Mainly interested in the role of conflict in stability and change. Offers insights into the adaptability of Western political and administrative institutions to non-Western societies.

354. Farris, George F. and D. Anthony Butterfield. "Control Theory in Brazilian Organizations." *Administrative Science Quarterly*, 17, 4 (December 1972), 574-585.

Measures the amount of "total control" and the distribution of control in sixteen Brazilian development banks to test hypotheses relating control to effectiveness. Uses Tannenbaum's "control graph method" as measure. Sample consists of 25 bank presidents and directors, 51 department chiefs, 43 technical supervisors, and 156 technical personnel. Concludes that greater control at each level is associated with increased effectiveness.

355. Fleming, William G. "Authority, Efficiency, and Role Stress: Problems in the Development of East African Bureaucracies." *Administrative Science Quarterly*, 11, 3 (December 1966), 386-404.

Suggests that East African colonial officers had a difficult time reconciling the competing needs of authority and efficiency in their administrative approaches. Different attempts to deal with this problem in Uganda, Tanganika, and Kenya demonstrated that in systems of indirect rule, there appeared to be a direct trade-off between the two commodities. Concludes that this trade-off was more apparent than real, however. Incompatibility was really a function of overemphasis on one goal or the other by colonial officials.

356. Fritz, Dan. "Bureaucratic Commitment in Rural India: A Psychological Application." *Asian Survey*, 16, 4 (April 1976), 338-354.

Assesses level of commitment to program
goals of Indian bureaucrats working on rural
development. Data based on interviews with 23
Block Development officers. Levels of commitment are seen as linked to Maslovian motivation theory. Noncommitted individuals are
those whose lower needs are not satisfied.
Concludes that enhancing growth of bureaucrats'
psychological needs will assist development.

357. Gitelman, Zvi and David Naveh. "Elite Accommodation and Organizational Effectiveness:
The Case of Immigrant Absorption in Israel."
Journal of Politics, 38, 4 (November 1976),
963-986.

Synthesizes Arendt Liphart's notion of elite
accommodation and Herbert Simon's view of
organizational behavior in an effort to develop
a model of organizational effectiveness. Presents in context of case study of the Israeli
Ministry of Immigrant Absorption. Finds that
this case underscores the importance of
organizational elites as a determinant of that
organization's effectiveness.

358. Goodsell, Charles T. "An Empirical Test of
'Legalism' in Administration." *Journal of
Developing Areas*, 10, 4 (April 1976), 485-
494.

Assesses the extent to which Latin American
bureaucracies are, as conventional wisdom has
it, plagued by an excess of rules, regulations,
statutes, and decrees. Reviews relevant
literature and tests proposition empirically
by comparing the operations of the postal services in the U.S. and Costa Rica. Opera-
tionalizes "legalism" by referring to rule
length, specificity, frequency of enforcement,
etc. Concludes that the idea that Latin
American societies are plagued by greater
legalism is completely false.

359. Greenwood, Royston, C.R. Hining and Stewart Ranson. "Contingency Theory and the Organization of Local Authorities: Part I. Differentiation and Integration." *Public Administration* (London), 53 (Spring 1975), 1-24.

Survey of 39 county authorities, 5 metropolitan county authorities, 33 metropolitan district authorities and 212 county district authorities in England and Wales in an effort to describe the organizational arrangements of new local authorities. Data are presented around the twin concepts of "differentiation" (organizational divisions) and "integration" (coordination of divisions). Continued with item 362.

360. Hanf, Kenneth. "Joint Decision-Making in the German Democratic Republic: An Interorganizational Perspective on Policy and Planning." *Organization and Administrative Sciences*, 8, 1 (Spring 1977), 41-61.

Begins with a review of the interorganizational theory literature, which has been developed largely in the context of Western pluralist societies. Applies this framework to the centralized system of the German Democratic Republic. This is appropriate, it is argued, because most scholars have under-emphasized the importance of horizontal organizational linkages in Eastern Europe. Analysis of the GDR is pitched at general level, with no specific case material provided.

*   Harris, Richard L. "The Effects of Political Change on the Role Set of the Senior Bureaucrats in Ghana and Nigeria." Cited as item 97.

361. Hiniker, Paul J. and Jolanta J. Perlstein. "Alternation of Charismatic and Bureaucratic Styles of Leadership in Postrevolutionary China." *Comparative Political*

Studies, 10, 4 (January 1978), 529-554.

Tests several hypotheses in an effort to
explain cycles of authority--Maoist to bureau-
cratic-pragmatic and back--in China. Suggests
that a simple Weberian model of leadership
provides the most accurate explanation.

362. Hinings, C.R., Royston Greenwood and Stewart
     Ranson. "Contingency Theory and the Organi-
     zation of Local Authorities: Part II. Con-
     tingencies and Structure." *Public Adminis-
     tration* (London), 53 (Summer 1975), 169-
     190.

     Continuation of item 359. Attempts to
     explain the pattern of similarities and
     differences observed in the structure of local
     authorities using a "contingency theory" frame-
     work. Contingency theory assumes that organi-
     zational structures are adaptations to environ-
     mental conditions. Look particularly at polit-
     ical control and managerial ideology as
     variables.

363. Hood, Christopher and Andrew Dunshire. *Bureau-
     metrics: The Quantitative Comparison of
     British Central Government Agencies*.
     University, Alabama: The University of
     Alabama Press, 1981.

     Develops an approach to studying organiza-
     tions quantitatively--"bureaumetics"--in an
     effort to assess similarities and differences
     between departments. Methodological in
     orientation. Three chapters present an appli-
     cation of the method in British central
     administration.

364. Hough, Jerry F. "The Bureaucratic Model and
     the Nature of the Soviet System." *Journal
     of Comparative Administration*, 5, 2 (August
     1973), 134-168.

Reviews attempts to apply Western theories and concepts of bureaucracy to the Soviet system. Finds support for parallels between industrial model and Soviet administration. One implication of this is that we need to break with the "directed society" paradigm of the Soviet Union and recognize the inherent pluralistic tendencies à la Cyert and March)

365. Kavcic, Bogden and Arnold S. Tannenbaum. "A Longitudinal Study of the Distribution of Control in Yugoslav Organizations." *Human Relations*, 34, 5 (1981), 397-417.

Examines the "actual" and "ideal" distribution of control in Yugoslav industrial organizations as reported by workers. Data drawn from 5 yearly surveys (1969-1973) of a sample of 3,000 people in 100 organizations. Period corresponds to new initiatives in worker self-management. Finds some shift toward real control within overall pattern of stability.

366. Langenderfer, Harold Q. "The Egyptian Executive: A Study in Conflict." *Human Organization*, 24, 1 (Spring 1965), 89-95.

Suggests that it is difficult to accelerate Egyptian economic development due to certain institutional and personal barriers in Egyptian management. These barriers are themselves products of the economic and cultural environment. Overall, political elites have paid too little attention to the need to develop human resources to stimulate economic growth.

367. Legendre, Pierre. "Lé Regime Historique des Bureaucraties Occidentales." *International Review of Administrative Sciences*, 38, 4 (1972), 361-378.

Examines two subjects--centralized management and adjustment to change--over time in

in the French case. Finds that contemporary
French centralization, though born of the
ancien regime, has been reinforced by many
occurrences since. Furthermore, French bureaucracy historically was far more capable of
adjusting to change than commonly thought.
Adaptation was possible mainly because
administrative elites, especially in the 19th
century, believed that any difficulties
could be overcome, as well as by international
professional contacts among higher civil servants.

*   Leonard, David K. *Reaching the Peasant Far-
      mer.* Cited as item 504.

368. Lewis-Beck, Michael S. "Influence Equality
      and Organizational Innovation in a Third
      World Nation: An Addictive-Nonaddictive
      Model." *American Journal of Political
      Science,* 21, 1 (February 1977), 1-12.

      Explores the relationship of equality in
      decisional influence on organizational inno-
      vation. Data based on random sample of 32
      Peruvian hospitals. Finds that influence
      equalization leads to innovation only when
      adequate resources are present.

369. Luckham, A.R. "Institutional Transfer and
      Breakdown in a New Nation: The Nigerian
      Military." *Administrative Science Quarterly,*
      16, 4 (December 1971), 387-406.

      Examines breakdown of discipline in Nigerian
      Army during the two coups of 1966 as a way
      to understand problems of creating new organi-
      zations in new nations. Stress put on high
      mobility rates, plus problem of reconciling
      primordial sentiments with organizational
      loyalties.

370. Lujan, Herman D. "The Bureaucratic Function
     and System Support: A Comparison of Guate-
     mala and Nicaragua." *Comparative Politics,*
     7, 4 (July 1975), 559-577.

     Sets forth a theoretical framework derived
     from systems analysis, and tests the effects
     of merged gatekeeping-output functions in
     bureaucracy using the cases of Guatemala and
     Nicaragua.

371. Magid, Alvin. "Dimensions of Administrative
     Role and Conflict Resolution Among Local
     Officials in Northern Nigeria." *Administra-
     tive Science Quarterly,* 12, 2 (September
     1967), 321-338.

     Tests the hypothesis that the person who
     feels an administrative role conflict will
     fill that role which he believes to be more
     legitimate or obligatory. Data drawn from
     interviews with 71 district councilors in
     Northern Nigeria. A high level of support is
     found for the hypothesis.

372. Magid, Alvin. *Man in the Middle: Leadership
     and Role Conflict in a Nigerian Society.*
     Manchester and New York: Manchester Univer-
     sity Press and African Publishing Co., 1976.

     Study of the "linkage positions"--chiefs,
     village headmen, and other local officials--
     that tie African tribal society to institu-
     tions of government. Applies role theory in
     an effort to understand pressures on these
     individuals. Case material drawn from Idoma,
     a village in South Central Nigeria. Includes
     appendices on interview schedule and tech-
     niques.

373. Markoff, John. "Governmental Bureaucratiza-
     tion: General Process and an Anomalous
     Case." *Comparative Studies in Society and
     History,* 17, 4 (October 1975), 479-503.

Begins with a review of theories of bureaucratization, including Weber's, Parson's, and
Michels'. Points out that most theories have
it that bureaucratization happens from above--
that government bureaucratizes itself. Too
often ignored is the fact that bureaucratization may be demanded from below. Examines
the Cahiers de Doléances de 1789 documents
produced in the course of the convocation of
1789, during the French revolution. They
present clear evidence of popular demands for
a more bureaucratic government.

374. Meillassoux, Claude. "A Class Analysis of
the Bureaucratic Process in Mali." *Journal
of Development Studies*, 6, 2 (January 1970),
97-110.

The pattern of dependency created by French
colonialism in Mali inhibited industrial
development and hence the formation of an
indigenous capitalist class at the same time
it fostered the growth of a large and domi-
neering bureaucracy. Although class analysis
is difficult in an African context, this
methodology needs to be used to understand
contemporary processes of development.

375. Milder, David N. "Some Aspects of Crozier's
Theory of Bureaucratic Organizations:
Charles DeGaulle as an Authoritarian
Reformer Figure." *Journal of Comparative
Administration*, 3, 1 (May 1971), 61-82.

Derives several hypotheses from Michel
Crozier's *The Bureaucratic Phenomenon* (item
346) regarding French leadership patterns and
tests them using survey data from the DeGaulle
era. Although some parts of Crozier's theory
are supported, one central element--the
influence of culture--is not. Crisis events
themselves, not generalized orientations
toward crises, influence the rise of authoritarian reformer figures in France.

376. Moore, Richard. "The Cross-Cultural Study
     of Organizational Behavior." *Human Organi-*
     zation, 33, 1 (Spring 1974), 37-46.

     Argues for a "culturally adjusted" approach
     to the study of organizational behavior. The
     human relations school and other similar
     approaches are either ethnocentric or lacking
     in comparative power.

377. Mosel, James N. "Fatalism in Thai Bureaucra-
     tice Decision-Making." *Anthropological*
     Quarterly, 39, 3 (July 1966), 191-199.

     Bureaucrats in Thailand have a more
     "fatalistic" outlook on life and their work
     than their Western counterparts. This is due
     to their perception that they are unlikely to
     be able to affect future events. Consequently,
     "coping" rather than "planning" strategies
     are adopted.

378. Nachmias, David and David H. Rosenbloom.
     "Antecedents of Public Bureaucracy: The
     Case of Israel." *Administration and Society,*
     9, 1 (May 1977), 45-80.

     Analyzes the propensity of bureaucrats to
     leave or "exit" public bureaucracies. Reports
     on research involving interviews with 630
     Israeli public servants. Concludes that turn-
     over can be decreased by fostering a more
     positive self-image among bureaucrats,
     reducing politicization, and adopting human
     relations techniques.

379. Odom, William E. *The Soviet Volunteers:*
     Modernization and Bureaucracy in a Public
     Mass Organization. Princeton: Princeton
     University Press, 1975.

     Historical study of the Osoviakhim, the
     Society of Friends of Defense and Aviation-
     Chemical Construction. Osoviakhim was an

enormous voluntary Soviet organization,
founded in 1927, that was coordinated by the
state to provide military training, marksman-
ship, aviation skills and so forth. Applies
Western organization theory--especially from
Merton, Selznick and Crozier--to understand
the behavior of Osoviakhim.

380. Oksenberg, M. "Methods of Communication
     Within the Chinese Bureaucracy." *The
     China Quarterly*, 57 (January/March 1974),
     1-39.

     Briefly reviews variety of communication
     methods within the Chinese bureaucracy and
     the importance attached to them. The methods
     include: meetings, work conferences, specialist
     meetings, symposia, informal discussions,
     transmission meetings, exchange of experience
     meetings, etc. Concludes with observations
     about changes in patterns, and geographic and
     organizational variations.

381. Pai-Panandiker, V.A. and S.S. Kshirsagar.
     "Bureaucracy in India: An Empirical Study."
     Indian Journal of Public Administration,
     17, 2 (April/June 1971), 187-208.

     Seeks to test extent to which the Indian
     bureaucracy conform to Weberian bureaucrat-
     ic theory. Data drawn from questionnaire
     given to 723 officials. Finds greater flexi-
     bility and adaptability in Indian bureaucracy,
     especially in developmentally oriented areas.

382. Poitras, Guy E. "Welfare Bureaucracy and
     Clientele Politics in Mexico." *Administra-
     tive Science Quarterly*, 18, 1 (March 1973),
     18-26.

     Welfare bureaucracies in developing coun-
     tries are supposed to pursue developmental as
     well as maintenance goals. The Mexican Social
     Security Institute is far more oriented toward
     stability than development, however. By

drawing into its structure representatives of
elite clientele members, and ignoring the
rank and file, the Institute has lost sight
of its goal of social change.

383. Prasad, G.K. *Bureaucracy in India: A Sociolo-
     gical Study.* New Delhi: Sterling Publishers
     PVT., Ltd., 1974.

     Empirical study of bureaucratic functions and
     dysfunctions in India. Based on documentary
     material and interviews with civil servants.
     Finds lack of correspondence between formal
     structure and actual decisional authority.
     Diffuse responsibility leads to noncreative
     and lax supervision. Large numbers of rules
     and procedures serve to buffer civil servants
     and to protect the bureaucratic system.

384. Rawin, Solomon John. "Social Values and the
     Managerial Structure." *Journal of Compara-
     tive Administration*, 2, 2 (August 1970),
     131-160.

     Compares socialist development in Poland
     and Yugoslavia. Although the Soviet model
     was common to both initially, little parallel
     development took place. Differences are
     ascribed largely to intrasystem forces--
     particularly social and cultural patterns
     from the pre-socialist past.

385. Richardson, J.J. "Agency Behaviour: The Case
     of Pollution Control in Sweden." *Public
     Administration* (London), 57 (Winter 1979),
     471-482.

     Despite Swedish cultural norms of ration-
     ality, deliberation and consensus which
     strengthen the autonomy of administrative
     agencies, experience with pollution control
     suggests that greater political control and
     coordination are needed. Reviews the legisla-
     tive and administrative context of Swedish

environmental policy. The greatest weakness lies in the area of enforcement. Organizations develop separate priorities and polluters are able to take advantage of competing agency goals.

386. Riggs, Fred W. "Organizational Structures and Contexts." *Administration and Society,* 7, 2 (August 1975), 150-190.

Proposes framework for comparative analysis based on structural characteristics of organizations. Types of organizations are constrained by environmental ecology and social context. An understanding of these factors may assist in the design of aid programs, which can be shaped to accord with the real possibilities of organizational types.

387. Roos , Leslie L. and Noralou P. Roos. "Bureaucracy in the Middle East: Some Cross-Cultural Relationships." *Journal of Comparative Administration,* 1, 3 (November 1969), 281-300.

Comparative analysis of bureaucracy in Turkey, Egypt and Pakistan. Provides secondary analysis of survey data in Egypt and Pakistan cases, and presents original data in Turkish case. Focuses on sources of job satisfaction and on likelihood of acquiescence in matters of conscience.

388. Scharpf, Fritz W. "Does Organization Matter? Task Structure and Interaction in the Ministerial Bureaucracy." *Organization and Administrative Sciences,* 8, 2-3 (Summer/Fall 1977), 149-168.

Discusses theoretical and methodological problems associated with a reorganization study of the West German Federal Ministry of Transport. Study had analyzed the internal structure of the Ministry to improve policy-

making capacity in the field of transportation. Found that organizational boundaries
can create barriers to information exchange,
which can impede policy coordination.

389. Schwartz, Donald V. "Decisionmaking,
Administrative Decentralization and Feed-
back Mechanisms: Comparison of Soviet and
Western Models." *Studies in Comparative
Communism,* 7, 1-2 (Spring/Summer 1974),
146-183.

Analyzes a cybernetic model of administration developed by V.G. Afansa'ev, a Soviet
scholar and Party official. Focuses on the
model's implications for administrative
decentralization and "feedback mechanisms."
Compares Afansa'ev's recommendations to Western
administrative practices, especially prefectoral systems, and argues that this model
amounts to a brief in favor of a strong,
active prefect.

390. Sheriff, Peta E. "Careers and the Organization: Locals and Cosmopolitans in the Higher
Civil Service." *International Review of
Administrative Sciences,* 41, 1 (1975),
29-36.

Argues that the traditional sociological concern with the influence of organizational
environments on career patterns needs to be
complemented by research into the reverse
relationships, namely the influence of careers
on organizational environments. Uses a case
study of the post-Fulton British senior civil
service to examine the effects of bringing a
group of people with very different career
orientations (specialists, in this case) into
an organization. Predicts that the vast
differences in career experiences will be
neutralized by the organization's environment.

*   Silberman, Bernard S. "Traditional Values
      or Organizational Imperatives in the
      Japanese Upper Civil Service." Cited as
      item 308.

391. Sivalingam, G. "The Relationship Between
      Leadership Style and Productivity in Two
      Agricultural Re-Development Schemes in
      West Malaysia." *Philippine Journal of
      Public Administration*, 19, 3 (July 1975),
      209-224.

      Studies effects of 11 leadership variables--
      consideration, upward and downward communica-
      tion, tolerance, superior orientation,
      initiating structure, psychological partici-
      pation, formal position, helpfulness, trust
      and respect--on agricultural productivity.
      Finds an interactive effect between leadership
      style and the personalities and social environ-
      ment of the settler farmers.

392. Springer, J. Fred and Richard W. Gable. "The
      Impact of Informal Relations on Organiza-
      tional Rewards: Comparing Bureaucracies in
      Southeast Asia." *Comparative Politics*, 12,
      2 (January 1980), 191-210.

      An empirical study of behavior in "informal"
      organizations--used in Barnard's sense--in
      Southeast Asia, based on a survey of 1,415
      public employees in Indonesia, the Philippines
      and Thailand. Tests what are termed the per-
      sonalist, dyadic and hierarchical models of
      informal relations that dominate the litera-
      ture. Concludes that personal ties as keys
      to bureaucratic success have been overempha-
      sized. Greater weight should be placed on
      the values, skills and procedures that emanate
      from the structure of the bureaucracy itself.

393. Strand, Torodd. "Expertise, Innovation, and
      Influence." *Scandinavian Political Studies*
      (1969), 117-132.

Focuses on the role of expert knowledge in
social change. Presents case material on
transportation planning in Oslo. Analyzes
professional ideologies and concludes with
scores of propositions about impact of
expertise on innovation.

*   Suleiman, Ezra N. "The Myth of Technical
     Expertise: Selection, Organization, and
     Leadership." Cited as item 321.

394. Tapia-Videla, Jorge I. "Understanding Organi-
     zations and Environments: A Comparative
     Perspective." *Public Administration Review,*
     36, 6 (November/December 1976), 631-636.

     Distinguishes between "macro" and "micro"
     levels of analysis. At macro level, there is
     a need to focus on the state and its relation-
     ship to the rest of society. Previous studies
     have ignored the extent to which the bureau-
     cracy is used as an instrument of ideological
     domination.

395. Tiger, Lionel. "Bureaucracy and Charisma in
     Ghana." *Journal of Asian and African
     Studies,* 1, 1 (January 1966), 13-26.

     Applies Weber's routinization of charisma
     hypothesis to the Nkrumah regime in Ghana.
     The move to Presidential leadership in 1960,
     the enlargement of Presidential control of
     crucial areas of government thereafter, and
     the general tendency toward centralization
     and specialization represented an effort to
     develop Ghana within a modern mold while
     preserving traditional elements. The civil
     service played a central role in this process.

396. Weaver, Jerry L. "Role Expectations of Latin
     American Bureaucrats." *Journal of Compara-
     tive Administration,* 4, 2 (August 1972),
     133-166.

Uses role theory to explain administrative behavior in Latin America. Summarizes several empirical studies undertaken by others, recasting in role framework. Includes work on Chile, Ecuador, Peru, Venezuela and Guatemala. Looks at social norms, ideology and organizational norms as major determinants.

*   Whyte, William F. "Imitation or Innovation: Reflections on the Institutional Development of Peru." Cited as item 552.

397. Zimbalist, Andrew. "The Dynamic of Worker Participation." *Administration and Society*, 7, 1 (May 1975), 43-54.

Presents analysis of survey of worker participation in 35 companies in Chile during the Allende period. Finds positive correlation between participation and productivity.

CHAPTER 7

PUBLIC BUDGETING

The field of budgeting is concerned principally with questions of public expenditure.
Although revenue questions are sometimes considered,
too, the main emphasis is on spending: How much
should be spent? What should it be spent on?
Especially important are questions about the way
budgetary decisions are made. For many years,
writers in the budgeting field have sought to
rationalize the budgeting process, to eliminate
extraneous (especially political) influences from
decision-making so that an optimum pattern of
expenditure can be produced. It has been this
search for rationality that has led to the systems
of budgeting, such as PPBS and RCB, described in
the works cited in this chapter. Whether these
systems have been successful is an open question,
one that provides a central focus for many of these
references.

398. Ames, Barry. "The Politics of Public Spending
     in Latin America." *American Journal of
     Political Science,* 21, 1 (February 1977),
     149-176.

     Presents a theory of public spending that
     hinges on the need to build political support
     through governmental expenditures. Tests by
     looking at patterns of spending of 17 Latin
     American central governments from 1948-1970.
     Finds that while resource availability is the
     best predictor of spending, civilian govern-
     ments respond to political demands of the
     electoral cycle and to constituency pressures.
     Military governments tend to spend a great
     deal initially and then to restrict outlays.

399. Bahry, Donna. "Measuring Communist Priorities: Budgets, Investments, and the Problem of Equivalence." *Comparative Political Studies*, 13, 3 (October 1980), 267-292.

    Argues that the peculiarities of communist budget presentations can lead to inaccurate conclusions when fiscal data are used without proper caution. Discusses several major studies that use quantitative fiscal analysis, reanalyzing the data. See items 404 and 466.

400. Balls, Herbert R. "Planning, Programming and Budgeting in Canada." *Public Administration* (London), 48 (Autumn 1970), 289-306.

    Describes PPBS implementation in Canada. Substantial progress has been made, though not all departments have fully implemented it. More emphasis has been placed on programming and budgeting than on planning and systems analysis.

401. Bourn, John. *Management in Central and Local Government*. London: Pitman Publishing, Ltd., 1979.

    General public administration text for Great Britain. Deals with specific management techniques, such as program budgeting, and cost-benefit analysis, as well as broad administrative issues in the British context. Includes overviews of major administrative reforms, such as the Fulton Report.

402. Bréaud, Patrick and Guy Braibant. "La Rationalisation des Choix Budgetaires." *International Review of Administrative Sciences*, 36, 4 (1970), 317-325.

    Two part article on French RCB. First section gives overview of system; second offers critical comments on initial operation. Problems identified include: meshing RCB with an administrative law system; defining the limits of RCB, especially in hard to quantify areas such as Foreign Affairs.

403. Bunce, Valerie. "Changing Leaders and Changing Policies: The Impact of Elite Succession on Budgetary Priorities in Democratic Countries." *American Journal of Political Science*, 24, 3 (August 1980), 373-395.

Analyzes the impact of electoral succession on budget allocations in seven advanced industrial nations (Austria, Britain, Canada, Federal Republic of Germany, Sweden, Japan and the U.S.) between 1950 and 1976. Finds no support for the hypothesis that elections do not disturb unilinear and incremental nature of budgets. Succession was found to be an important political variable that shapes budgets across time and across nations.

404. Bunce, Valerie. "Measuring Communist Priorities: A Reply to Bahry." *Comparative Political Studies*, 13, 3 (October 1980), 293-298.

Defends analysis of communist budgets against Bahry criticisms (item 399). Argues that inconsistencies in statistical reporting discussed by Bahry can be treated in other ways. See items 399 and 466.

405. Buscema, S. "Problèmes Actuels du Budget de l'Etat." *International Review of Administrative Sciences*, 37, 1-2 (1971), 22-37.

Broad discussion of budget problems in Italy. Among the difficulties identified are: (1) budget fragmentation, whereby the state budget document incompletely reflects the full range of public spending; (2) lack of coordination between national, regional and local levels; (3) inadequate classification procedures; and (4) off-budget expenditures.

406. Caiden, Naomi. "Budgeting in Poor Countries:
     Ten Assumptions Re-examined." *Public
     Administration Review*, 40, 1 (January/
     February 1980), 40-46.

     Critically assesses ten common assumptions
     made by those who try to write about budget
     processes in less developed countries. These
     assumptions range from the idea that there is
     a common pattern of budgeting that will fit
     all circumstances to the belief that budget-
     ing is relevant to development. None of
     these assumptions is wholly accurate. Sug-
     gestions are made for improving professional
     advice about budgeting in poor countries.

407. Caiden, Naomi and Aaron Wildavsky. *Planning
     and Budgeting in Poor Countires*. New York:
     John Wiley, 1974.

     The paradox of developing countries is that
     the very pressing need they have for sophisti-
     cated, efficiency-maximizing resource alloca-
     tion processes is exactly what prevents them
     from adopting them. Planning and long-range
     budgeting systems are forestalled by inadequate
     infrastructures and high levels of uncertainty.
     Budgeting in the countries of the developing
     world tends to be especially incremental and
     repetitive. Offers suggestions for more
     appropriate responses to the administrative
     needs of these nations.

408. Campbell, John Creighton. *Contemporary
     Japanese Budget Politics*. Berkeley: Univer-
     sity of California Press, 1977.

     General description of Japanese budgeting.
     Discusses the role of the Ministry of Finance,
     the spending ministries and the parliament
     (specifically members of the ruling Liberal
     Democratic Party). Provides detailed informa-
     tion on budget types and decisional strategies.
     Also includes an historical overview of the
     evolution of the budgetary system. Some

statistical material presented.

409. Coskun, Gulay. "Budget Reform in the Republican Government of Turkey." *International Review of Administrative Sciences,* 37, 4 (1971), 330-336.

Assistant Director of the Turkish Budget Department describes budgeting problems in Turkey, and outlines reforms. Program budgeting is seen as the chief remedy to the weaknesses of the traditional line-item approach. No results of the reform are reported, as it was not fully implemented at the time. An appendix to the article contains the directive of the Prime Minister requiring that program budgeting be installed.

410. Cowart, Andrew T. "Partisan Politics and the Budgetary Process in Oslo." *American Journal of Political Science,* 19, 4 (November 1975), 651-666.

Tests two models of political effects on budgeting: party program model and alliance structure model. Data drawn from interviews with agency officials in the Oslo municipal government. Party support and alliance structures are found to have great effect on budget success of agencies at all levels of the process.

411. Cowart, Andrew T., Tore Hansen and Karl-Erik Brofoss. "Budgetary Strategies and Success at Multiple Decision Levels in the Norwegian Urban Setting." *American Political Science Review,* 69, 2 (June 1975), 543-558.

Quantitative tests of various budget decision models are presented using data drawn from budget decisions for forty-seven agencies over a nineteen year period in Oslo. Concludes that "acquisitiveness" of agency budget strategies most important determinant of budget growth.

412. Danziger, James N. "Assessing Incrementalism
     in British Municipal Budgeting." *British
     Journal of Political Science,* 6, 3 (July
     1976), 335-350.

     Sets forth several operational models of
     budgetary incrementalism and tests them
     empirically using data drawn from British
     county borough expenditures. Notes that pre-
     dictive power varies with circumstances. The
     "incremental trend" model and "base budget"
     model provide the best overall estimates of
     outputs.

413. Danziger, James N. *Making Budgets: Public
     Resource Allocation.* Beverly Hills: Sage
     Publications, 1978.

     Systematic empirical analysis of alternative
     theories of budget outcomes. Data drawn from
     interviews with budget makers and from budget
     documents in British county government. Con-
     cludes that extant theories, given present
     level of knowledge, must be seen as complemen-
     tary rather than competing.

414. de la Genière, Renaud. *Le Budget.* Paris:
     Presses de la Fondation Nationale des
     Science Politiques, 1976.

     Detailed technical treatment of French budg-
     et process by the Director of the Bank of
     France. Explains the variety of French budg-
     ets--white, blue, yellow, green--and the
     purposes to which they are put and by whom.

415. d'Eszlary, Charles. "Les Administrations
     Camérales de Brandebourg et de la Monarchie
     des Habsbourg et leurs Effets sur les
     Administrations Modernes." *International
     Review of Administrative Sciences,* 30,
     2 (1964), 171-178.

     Describes transition from tax farming to
     direct government collection of revenues in

Brandenburg and Hapsburg in the 16th and 17th
centuries. Also discusses evolution of
treasuries, with rudimentary balancing of
receipts and expenditures. The roots of
modern public budgeting and accounting are to
be found here.

416. Doh, Joon Chien. "Conceptual Framework of an
Integrated Approach to Budgeting for the
ESCAP Countires." *International Review of
Administrative Sciences*, 43, 2 (1977), 141-
152.

Argues that since budgeting has a "moral
responsibility to the poor" the thirty-plus
countries and territories of the Economic
and Social Commission for Asia and the Pacific
need to rethink their systems of financial
planning along the lines outlined here, a
modified form of program budgeting.

417. Ducros, Jean-Claude. "La Rationalisation des
Choix Budgetaires et l'Organisation de
l'Administration." *International Review
of Administrative Sciences*, 39, 1 (1973),
25-48.

Analyzes the Rationalization of Budgetary
Choices (RCB) system in France, the equivalent
of the American PPBS. Discusses the effects
on centralization/decentralization of decision-
making, as well as problems of specialization
and coordination. Concludes that RCB will
restrict the autonomy of agencies while at
the same time permitting some deconcentration
of power to the field.

418. Dyson, K.H.F. "Planning and the Federal
Chancellor's Office in the West German
Federal Government." *Political Studies*,
21, 3 (September 1973), 348-362.

Notes that social and economic planning in
Germany has been incremental and reactive.
It is seen as necessary, but ideologically

suspect. Added to these difficulties are
serious organizational problems. Rampant
departmentalism has weakened the central
planning staff located in the Chancellor's
office.

419. Echols, John M. "Politics, Budgets, and
     Regional Equality in Communist and Capitalist
     Systems." *Comparative Political Studies*,
     8, 3 (October 1975), 259-292.

     Sets out to determine empirically differences
     between communist and capitalist regimes on
     the issue of areal inequality using budget
     data. U.S. and Soviet Union are the foci of
     analysis, though inference is made to other
     systems. Concludes that the existence of
     inequality is not solely an objective matter,
     that attitudes must be taken into account.

420. Fernandez, Felisa D. "The Budget Process and
     Economic Development: The Philippine
     Experience." *Philippine Journal of Public
     Administration*, 16, 1 (January 1972), 58-72.

     Describes the evolution of Filipino budget-
     ing procedures, with a focus on institutions,
     concepts, and budget formats. Includes a dis-
     cussion of PPBS efforts.

421. Galnoor, Itzhak. "Reforms of Public Expendi-
     ture in Great Britain." *Canadian Public
     Administration*, 17, 2 (Summer 1974), 289-
     320.

     British budgetary system breaks process down
     into three elements: (1) macro-budgeting,
     setting five year projections by area of out-
     lay (Public Expenditure Survey); (2) micro-
     budgeting, analyzing ministerial activities
     (Programme Analysis and Review); and (3)
     policy analysis, scrutinizing the effects of
     policy on public expenditures (Central Policy
     Review Staff).

422. Garcia-Quintana, César A. "La Constitución
    Espanola y el Presupuesto del Estado."
    *International Review of Administrative
    Sciences*, 46, 1 (1980), 23-34.

    Discusses the budgetary process under the
    1978 Spanish constitution. Concentrates on
    legal provisions.

423. Greenwood, Royston, C.R. Hinings and Stewart
    Ranson. "The Politics of the Budgetary
    Process in English Local Government."
    Political Studies, 25, 1 (March 1977), 25-
    47.

    Elaborates a general theory of the budgetary
    process that seeks to move beyond incremental-
    ism as an explanation of outcomes. Organi-
    zational politics rather than limited rational-
    ity is the central focus of the theory.
    Theory illustrated with data drawn from a
    sample of the budgets of 27 local authorities
    in Great Britain.

424. Groenewegan, P.D. "The Australian Budget
    Process." *Public Administration* (Sydney),
    22, 3 (September 1973), 251-267.

    Describes the budget timetable and budget
    estimate preparation procedure in Australia.
    Concludes that the annual budget has considera-
    ble disadvantages. Recommends change in time-
    table, reduction in secrecy and publication of
    the Treasury's economic forecast.

425. Guruprasad, C. "Planning for Tax Administra-
    tion in Canada." *Canadian Public Adminis-
    tration*, 16, 3 (Fall 1973), 399-421.

    Study of PPB implementation in the Depart-
    ment of National Revenue and Taxation in
    Canada. Notes obstacles to implementation that
    stemmed from organizational incapacities and
    Treasury Board exigencies. Suggests that
    existing techniques and PPB systems need to

be synthesized to allow for smooth transition.

426. Handa, K.L. "Budget Management Techniques:
     A Perspective for India." *Indian Journal
     of Public Administration,* 26, 3 (July/
     September 1980), 648-662.

     Systematically discusses applicability of
     line-item, performance, program, and zero-base
     budgeting techniques in Indian context. Pro-
     vides historical background on expenditure
     system in India. Suggests that only perform-
     ance budgeting is feasible. Line-item is too
     control-oriented, while PPB and ZBB require
     too much planning and analysis.

427. Hartley, Keith. "Programme Budgeting and the
     Economics of Defense." *Public Administra-
     tion* (London), 52 (Spring 1974), 55-72.

     Examines reforms in British defense budget-
     ing procedures in the 1964-72 period, many
     of which parallel those in the U.S. Includes
     data illustrating "functional" approach to
     defense budgeting. Concludes that the pro-
     gramme system is useful for stimulating
     "clearer thinking" about aims and costs, but
     cannot answer the question, how large should
     the budget be?

428. Heclo, Hugh and Aaron Wildavsky. *The Private
     Government of Public Money.* Berkeley:
     University of California Press, 1974).

     Analyzes the politics of the budgetary
     process in Great Britain. Describes roles
     and strategies of major participants--the
     Treasury, ministries, the Cabinet, and members
     of parliament. Treats three major reforms
     of the late 1960's: the Public Expenditure
     Survey, Programme Analysis and Review, and
     the Central Policy Review Staff.

429. Hettlage, Karl M. "The Problems of Medium-
     term Financial Planning." *Public Administra-
     tion* (London), 48 (Autumn 1970), 263-272.

     Discusses the objectives and development of
     financial planning in the German Federal
     Republic. Budget procedures are briefly de-
     scribed and the special problems posed by
     Germany's federal structure are addressed.

430. Higley, John, Karl Erik Brofoss, and Knut
     Groholt. "Top Civil Servants and the
     National Budget in Norway." *The Mandarins
     of Western Europe: The Political Role of
     Top Civil Servants* (item 91).

     Relations between politicians and civil
     servants in Norway are marked by cooperation
     and harmony, rather than by conflict and dis-
     cord. A case study of national budget-making
     is presented to illustrate these dynamics.
     The main reason for good relations among
     elites is the fact that civil servants are
     not viewed as threats to the status of polit-
     ical elites.

431. Huet, Phillippe. "The Rationalization of
     Budget Choices in France." *Public Adminis-
     tration* (London), 48 (Autumn 1970), 273-
     288.

     Article by Director-General of the French
     Ministry of Economic Affairs and Finance
     describes the RCB system adopted in France.
     Some of the difficulties of application are
     outlined.

432. Huet, Phillippe and Jacques Bravo. *L'Expéri-
     ence Française de Rationalisation des
     Choix Bugetaires.* Paris: Presses Universi-
     taires de France, 1973.

     Survey of French attempt to adopt RCB.
     Includes history of reform (by Huet) and a

detailed explanation of the technique (by
Bravo). Concludes with case studies of RCB
implementation in three ministries.

433. Ivarsson, Sven I. "Effets de l'Informatique
     et du Budget-Programme sur l'Administration
     Publique." *International Review of Adminis-
     trative Sciences*, 36, 2 (1970), 115-121.

     Examines the effects of automatic data
     processing and program budgeting on public
     administration in Sweden. Notes that the
     Swedes built their PPB system from the bottom
     up, rather than from the top down, as in the
     U.S. The effects on the agencies have been
     varied. Debates about goals and duties have
     occurred, planning has been enhanced, and
     decisions have been more rational.

434. Jacqumotte, J.P. "Tentative Comparative
     Study of RCB in France and PPBS in Belgium."
     *International Review of Administrative
     Sciences*, 36, 1 (1970), 47-55.

     Compares the RCB system in France with the
     Belgium PPBS endeavor. The aims of the two
     efforts are the same, though the systems
     differ. The French RCB is linked to a more
     comprehensive national plan, though taken
     alone, PPBS is itself more comprehensive.
     Concludes with speculation that these reforms
     will have salutary effects in these two
     administrative law countries, for it will mean
     an injection of a new concern for relevance.

435. Jaliff, Isidoro. "Algunas Reflexiones Acerca
     del Conjunto 'Planificaión-Presupuesto por
     Programas' en la Reforma Administrativa."
     *International Review of Administrative
     Sciences*, 39, 2 (1973), 108-118.

     Outlines basic PPB techniques and proceeds
     to an analysis based on the Latin American
     experience. Recommends better coordination,
     strengthened intermediate-range planning and

increased participation of line agencies.

436. Jochimsen, Reimut. "Problems of Establishing
an Integrated Planning System for Goal-
Setting and Co-ordination within the Federal
Government." *International Review of
Administrative Sciences*, 38, 2 (1972), 181-
192.

Reviews the current state of fiscal planning in the West German Federal government,
and finds it wanting. Outlines several
alternative directions that planning could
take. Also discusses the problems involved
in coordinating Federal action with the Lander
(states).

437. Johnson, A.W. "The Treasury Board of Canada
and the Machinery of Government of the
1970's." *Canadian Journal of Political
Science*, 4, 3 (September 1971), 346-366.

Describes the "new" Treasury Board of Canada
and its present functions. The Treasury Board
is the cabinet body that acts as budget
compiler and administrative overseer of the
Canadian federal government. Notes greater
openness and broader ministerial participation
in its activities. Argues that bureaucratic
and public perceptions of its functions need
to come into line with these new realities.

438. Kabir, A.K.M. and Md. Anisuzzaman. "Performance Budgeting: Its Application in Pakistan." *International Review of Administrative Sciences*, 33, 4 (1967), 345-355.

Close association between American universities and Pakistani officials has influenced
budgetary concepts in Pakistan. Performance
budgeting was first officially urged in the
*Report of the Provincial Reorganization Com-
mittee* in 1961, which led to the establishment
of a Budget Reform Committee (BRC) in 1962.

The BRC's report in 1965 urged the adoption of performance budgeting, a recommendation that has been accepted by the government but not yet fully implemented.

439. Klein, Rudolf. "The Politics of PPB." *Political Quarterly*, 43, 3 (July/September 1972), 270-281.

New techniques like PPB need to be scrutinized closely, for they produce different decisions, not just better decisions. Explains how PPB works and discusses in the context of a British feasibility study in the Department of Education and Science. Points out various problems with actually using technique. Believes that implementation will entail an even greater shift of power away from the House of Commons to the bureaucracy.

440. Kobzina, Alfred. "Considérations sur le Budget Autrichien." *International Review of Administrative Sciences*, 28, 2 (1962), 133-145.

Outlines Austrian budget procedure. Discusses the Federal Finance Act of 1962, which is the basis of all current financial administration. Notes that Ministry of Finance responsible for overall budget preparation and execution, although close scrutiny is exercised by the National Assembly.

441. Kone, A. "L'Administration du Budget en Côte d'Ivoire." *International Review of Administrative Sciences*, 43, 2 (1977), 102-104.

Describes the structure of the Ivorian budget and the process by which it is assembled. Emphasizes legal points.

442. Kureisky, M.A. "Reforms in Financial Management in Pakistan." *International Review of
Administrative Sciences,* 39, 3 (1973), 235-
246.

Reviews budgeting, expenditure and auditing
procedures in Pakistan. Argues that the system is now outdated, and needs wholesale
revision to keep pace with Pakistani development. In particular, calls for a consolidated
"Code of Accounts" and full pre-audit.

443. Kwang, Ching-wen. "The Budgetary System of
the People's Republic of China: A Preliminary Survey." *Public Finance,* 18, 3-4
(1963), 253-283.

After a brief institutional description of
mainland Chinese governmental institutions,
discusses system of financial administration,
including process of budget preparation,
center-local fiscal relations, legislative
review, auditing, and tax administration.
Concludes with an analysis of budget classification and structure, accompanied by data
for fiscal years 1950-1960.

444. Lord, Guy. *The French Budgetary Process.*
Berkeley: University of California Press,
1973.

General description of French budgetary
system from an administrative and political
perspective. Research based on 1960's period,
and hence excludes consideration of Rationalisation des Choix Budgetaires (RCB). Covers
history of French budgeting, constitutional
and financial context, actors, attitudes and
strategies.

445. Murphy, Marvin. "Budget Reform in the
Republic of Vietnam." *International Review
of Administrative Sciences,* 26, 2 (1960),
357-363.

Member of the Michigan State University
Vietnamese Advisory Group describes effort
to remodel Vietnam's budget process along
functional lines, centralizing more authority
in the office of the president. Prior to this
time, the budget was little more than an
accounting device.

446. Murray, Carl A. "Classical Principles in
    Modern Government Budgeting." *International
    Review of Administrative Sciences*, 36, 2
    (1970), 109-114.

    Since the early 19th century, budget-makers
    in almost all countries have accepted certain
    basic principles to guide their action:
    universality and unity, limitation of budget
    period to fixed time, and systematic item
    classification. These principles are illustra-
    ted by reference to the Swedish case.

447. Neumann, R.W. "Introducing Programme Budget-
    ing in Norway." *International Review of
    Administrative Sciences*, 37, 3 (1971), 403-
    410.

    Consists largely of general explanation of
    program budgeting. No specific references to
    how system actually works in Norway, though
    elaborate diagnoses are provided.

448. Ohkawa, Masazo. "PPBS in Japan--Technical
    and Political Problems." *Public Finance*,
    27, 2 (1972), 212-216.

    PPBS is not yet implemented in Japanese
    government, although extensive preparation and
    planning have taken place. Anticipated prob-
    lems include the difficulty of making quanti-
    tative assessments of social programs, an
    overemphasis on efficiency, lack of analysts
    and interministerial coordination. Political
    problems may also arise given the power posi-
    tion of the administrative elite and the role

of opposition political parties.

449. Ola, R.O.F. "Two Commonwealth Watchdogs: A Comparative Study of the Evolution and Position of the Audtors-General of Nigeria and Canada." *International Review of Administrative Sciences*, 45, 1 (1979), 35-40.

Although both Canada and Nigeria share the Commonwealth tradition, borrowed from Britain, of using an auditor-general to ensure financial accountability, the Canadian office is older and more institutionalized.

450. Peterson, A.W. "Planning, Programming and Budgeting in the 'GLC'." *Public Administration* (London), 50 (Summer 1972), 119-126.

Description of efforts to apply PPBS technology in Greater London Council decision-making by the GLC Director-General. Conceded that it has not yet worked completely, but argues that many advantages have already been reaped.

451. Pisotine, M.I. "Les Nouvelles Techniques de Préparation et d'Améngement du Budget en U.R.S.S." *International Review of Administrative Sciences*, 32, 1 (1966), 10-22.

Argues that Soviet budgeting, a critical element in socialist economic planning, has recently been improved. Describes the steps in the process, from budget preparation through budget authorization to budget execution.

452. Pollitt, Christopher. "The Political Administration of Economic Decline: British Central Government Since the 1960's." *Public Administration Review*, 41, 5 (September/October 1981), 514-519.

Describes British economic management during
the 1970's, drawing parallels with U.S. Notes
end of 1960's optimism about rational planning
and resource allocation. Includes statistics
on public expenditures and employment.

453. Pollitt, Christopher. "The Public Expenditure
Survey, 1961-72." *Public Administration*
(London), 55 (Summer 1977), 127-142.

Historical review of the first ten years of
the British Public Expenditure Survey (PESC),
which is the system used to plan and control
central government spending. Identifies the
major political, economic and organizational
issues in various stages of PESC's development.

454. Preece, R.J.C. "The Budget as Law in the
German Federal Republic." *Political
Studies*, 16, 1 (March 1968), 94-96.

Discusses the legal status of administrative
budgets in West Germany, noting the ambiguity
that reigned prior to a 1966 decision of the
Federal Constitutional Court. It is now clear
that, unlike Switzerland, where budgets are
considered purely "internal expedients,"
German budgets are matters of law, as in
Britain and the U.S.

455. Questiaux, Pauli. "Les Nouvelles Techniques
de Preparation et d'Aménagement du Budget en
France." *International Review of Administrative Sciences*, 31, 4 (1965), 310-329.

Finance inspector describes stages of French
budget preparation. The process is simplified
by using the device of "voted services"--
80-95% of all appropriations are continued
without review. Only new items receive close
scrutiny.

456. Richardson, Ivan L. "Municipal Government in
     Brazil: The Financial Dimension." *Journal
     of Comparative Administration*, 1, 3
     (November 1969), 321-344.

     Brazilian government in general, and the
     financial system in particular, has become far
     more centralized since the 1964 revolution.
     Municipalities now have little autonomy in
     generating their own revenues. The federal
     government is likened to a "puppeteer" pull-
     ing the strings of over 4,000 municipalities.

457. Ridler, Neil B. "PPB--Its Relevance to
     Financially Constrained Municipalities."
     Canadian Public Administration, 19, 2
     (Summer 1976), 238-253.

     Starts with the assumption that PPB is
     preferable to traditional budgeting. However,
     the ability of Canadian municipalities to
     adopt this procedure is constrained by fiscal
     imbalance. In particular, a reliance on
     intergovernmental transfers and the property
     tax has distorted priorities and narrowed
     decision-making. Inflation has aggravated the
     problem. Offers some suggestions to get PPBS
     in place.

458. Rodríguez Aznar, José Vincente. "La Programa-
     ción de Presupuestas Sectoriales, un Nuevo
     Método Presupuestario en la Administración
     Publica." *International Review of Adminis-
     trative Sciences*, 38, 3 (1972), 277-282.

     Reviews Latin American experience with
     program budgeting. Notes difficulty meshing
     national development plan with program budg-
     ets. Argues for sectoral programming of
     budgets to help bridge the gap.

459. Saetersdal, Olaf. "Norwegian Experiences in
     the Application of New Budgetary Methods."
     Public Finance, 27, 2 (1972), 217-221.

PPBS in Norway is viewed as a system of many parts, each of which can be accepted on its own without necessarily buying the whole package. So far, the Norwegian government has reclassified expenditures into program categories, introduced multi-year budgeting and adopted some quantitative analytical techniques.

460. Sandberg, M. and H. Stoessel. "Budget Preparation and Management in Israel." *International Review of Administrative Sciences*, 31, 4 (1965), 330-346.

Director and Deputy Director of Budgets outline Israeli budget procedures. Arranged as answers to questions posed by an International Institute of Administrative Sciences survey.

461. Segsworth, R.V. "PPBS and Policy Analysis: The Canadian Experience." *International Review of Administrative Sciences*, 38, 4 (1972), 419-426.

Reviews events leading up to adoption of PPBS in Canada, and examines whether this system can be applied to policy analysis. Concludes that system has not been adopted in its entirety, owing (1) to lack of qualified staff; (2) to political naivete of economists; and (3) to resistance by operating departments. However, the partial form that has survived is viewed as a quite useful compromise between rationality and political expedience.

462. Shand, D.A. "The Forward Planning of Public Expenditure." *New Zealand Journal of Public Administration*, 33, 1 (September 1970), 8-29.

Focuses on major developments in budget administration and financial planning in the United Kingdom in the 1960's, with some reference to parallel developments in New Zealand. Discusses the Plowden Committee

Report (1961), the Green Paper (1969), and the
Public Expenditure Survey Committee (1969).
New Zealand can learn from these British reforms, since existing procedures contain the
old British deficiencies.

463. Soberano, Jose D. "Tax Structure and Adminis-
    tration." *Philippine Journal of Public
    Administration*, 11, 2 (April 1967), 98-107.

    After defining basic concepts in tax
    administration, discusses revenue structure in
    the Philippines. Explains procedures for tax
    assessment, collection and enforcement.

464. Strick, J.C. "Recent Developments in Canadian
    Financial Administration." *Public Adminis-
    tration* (London), 48 (Spring 1970), 69-85.

    Analyzes changes in Canadian financial
    administration in the years following the 1962
    Report of the Royal Commission on Government
    Organization. The major emphasis is on new
    quantitative approaches to budgeting and
    financial management, including PPBS, coupled
    with greater decentralization from the Trea-
    sury Board to departments.

465. Vasquez de Prada, V.R. "La Administración
    Financiera Española." *International Review
    of Administrative Sciences*, 35, 2-3 (1969),
    210-217.

    Outlines the history of Spanish financial
    administration, with an emphasis on the role
    of current Ministry of Finance. Describes
    the results of the 1968 decree which reorgani-
    zed the Ministry and defined its responsibili-
    ties.

466. Welsh, William A. "On Understanding Budgets and Public Expenditures in Eastern Europe: A Reply to Bahry." *Comparative Political Studies*, 10, 3 (October 1980), 299-308.

    Argues that Bahry's (item 399) discussion of the problems of budget analysis useful but incompletely developed. Many of the difficulties she identifies have in fact been addressed in the research she reanalyzes. Moreover, she overstresses the overall seriousness of the problem. See item 404.

467. Wildavsky, Aaron. *Budgeting: A Comparative Theory of Budgetary Processes*. Boston: Little-Brown, 1975.

    Broadranging collection of insights into budgetary processes, with illustrations drawn from developing and developed countries. Specifically, among developed nations, U.S., Britain, and France received detailed discussions. Basically an elaboration of Wildavsky's incrementalist model, complete with attacks on program budgeting and other budgetary reforms.

468. Wildavsky, Aaron. "Why Planning Fails in Nepal." *Administrative Science Quarterly*, 17, 4 (December 1972), 508-528.

    Planning in Nepal does not work; money allocated doesn't get spent; targets set don't get met. Reviews the reasons typically put forth for failure of planning--insufficient information, bad project proposals, inability to administer foreign aid, and opposition of the finance ministry--and concludes that the problem is planning itself. Nepal is simply ill-suited, due to lack of infrastructure, to plan.

469. Wright, Maurice. "Public Expenditure in
Britain: The Crisis of Control." *Public
Administration* (London), 55 (Summer 1977),
143-169.

The British Public Expenditure Survey
(PESC), after ten years of relatively smooth
development, has moved into a "state of deep
crisis." The weakness of the British economy
accounts for some of the problem, but even
more important are structural weaknesses within PESC itself. Chief among these is its
failure to plan for inflation, and to control
monetary costs. The introduction of cash
limits in 1975 has helped, although it is
difficult to predict PESC's fate.

470. Yoingco, Angel Q. Antonio O. Casem, Jr. and
Amancia G. Laureta. "A Review of the
Philippine Experience in Performance Budg-
eting." *Philippine Journal of Public
Administration,* 13, 3 (July 1969), 263-
274.

Reports survey of 36 Philippine budget officers and their attitudes toward performance
budgeting. Notes that most consider it very
successful, although specific reforms are
suggested.

CHAPTER 8

DEVELOPMENT ADMINISTRATION

Development administration is an area of comparative public administration that focuses on the special problems and possibilities of administrative systems in the poor countries of the world. The term development administration has come to mean both attempts to upgrade ("develop") administration in third world countries and efforts to create unique (development-oriented) administrative systems especially equipped to spur economic growth. Both uses are represented in the references included in this chapter.

471. Adamolekun, Ladip. "Towards Development-Oriented Bureaucracies in Africa." *International Review of Administrative Sciences*, 42, 3 (1976), 256-265.

Development-oriented bureaucracies will not come about until three requirements are met: (1) committed political leadership; (2) internalized norms of public service among bureaucrats; (3) establishment of permanent machinery for administrative reform. Illustrations are drawn from the experiences of Tanzania, Nigeria, Senegal, and the Lusophone states.

472. Al-Araji, A.M. "'Non-Planning' Approach in Administrative Development Policy-Making in Iraq." *International Review of Administrative Sciences* 43, 4 (1977), 357-364.

Compares pre-1972 period of non-planning with post-1972 planning era in effort to

assess impact of these two approaches. Concludes that the "planning approach" has helped
accomplish the goals of the 1972 National
Development Plan.

473. Aquino, Belinda A. "Dimensions of Develop-
     ment in Philippine Provinces, 1970."
     Philippine Journal of Public Administration,
     19, 1-2 (January/April 1975), 15-45.

     Identifies five measures of development--
     urbanization, rural employment, landlordism,
     migration and economic activity--and ranks
     Philippine provinces accordingly. Notes that
     this ranking is only suggestive due to the
     aggregate nature of the date.

474. Braibanti, Ralph. *Research on the Bureaucracy
     of Pakistan*. Durham: Duke University Press,
     1966.

     Comprehensive research guide to Pakistani
     public administration. Begins with an over-
     view of the research environment (access
     problems, language difficulties, etc.) and
     presents a history of bureaucracy in Pakistan,
     integrating all relevant source material.
     Subsequent chapters on local government,
     administrative reform, legal research, and so
     forth follow the same pattern, outlining major
     issues while weaving in a guide to sources.
     Includes fifteen appendices, ranging from
     politicians' speeches to extracts from the
     reports of government commissions.

475. Brown, Richard H. "Toward a Communalist
     Approach to National Development Planning."
     Public Administration Review, 38, 3 (May/
     June 1978), 262-267.

     Argues that capital- and technology-intensive
     approaches to development are misplaced. They
     fail to utilize the major resources of most
     poor countries--manpower, simple skills, and

local materials. Suggests local level
"populist mobilization" as the key to successful development.

476. Cariño, Ledivina V. "Bureaucratic Norms,
Corruption, and Development." Philippine
Journal of Public Administration, 19, 3
(October 1975), 278-292.

Although Philippine bureaucrats have partial-
ly internalized Weberian norms of conduct,
corruption remains a problem. Article discusses possible causes and effects of corruption. Illustrates with a case study of the
Philippine Bureau of Resource Management.

477. Coward, E. Walter. "Indigenous Organisation,
Bureaucracy and Development: The Case of
Irrigation." Journal of Development Studies,
13, 1 (October 1976), 92-105.

Typically large-scale irrigation projects
experience difficulties of communication
between program administrators and water
users. One solution to this problem is the
adaptation of indigenous irrigation leadership roles as a link between bureaucracy and
consumers. Presents case material of such
successful adaptation in Western Laos.

478. Daland, Robert T. Brazilian Planning:
Development Politics and Administration.
Chapel Hill: University of North Carolina
Press, 1967.

Asks: Is planning necessary, desirable or
possible in developing countries? Believes
asserted linkage between planning and development not yet established. Tries to answer
through case analysis of twenty years of
Brazilian planning efforts. Concludes that
while plan preparation assists regime survi-
val, plan implementation has negative consequences on this dimension. Thus, the

linkage between planning and development is neither direct nor uniformly positive.

479. Daland, Robert T. "Development Administration and the Brazilian Political System." *Western Political Quarterly*, 21, 2 (June 1968), 325-339.

Uses Riggs's 'prismatic' framework to analyze Brazilian administration. Hypothesizes that a prismatic system with a non-consensual elite and a history of instability must decentralize programs to engender participation in development.

480. Deva, Satya. "Western Conceptualization of Administrative Development: A Critique and an Alternative." *International Review of Administrative Sciences*, 45, 1 (1979), 59-63.

Argues that development administration, as conventionally understood in the West, has its roots in American anti-communism of 1950's, and provides an inappropriate framework for administration in the Third World. Offers alternative scheme built around values of decentralization, anti-corruption, economic equality, and political participation.

481. Diamant, Alfred. "European Models of Bureaucracy and Development." *International Review of Administrative Sciences*, 32, 4 (1966), 309-320.

After tracing the "basic pattern" of European modernization, looks at social, economic, political, and bureaucratic dimensions of development. Suggests that while Europe offers no necessary normative guide to contemporary developing nations, important historical lessons can be learned. Concludes with an assessment of the relevance of current Western administrative and organization theory for new nations, which is found to be

insufficient, in part because it is too pre-
occupied with the maintenance of equilibrium.

482. Dresang, Dennis L. "Entrepreneurialism and
Development Administration." *Administrative
Science Quarterly*, 18, 1 (March 1973), 76-
85.

Suggests that one explanation for the occa-
sional success of development projects is the
activity of entrepreneurial bureaucrats who
seek to enhance their career advancement by
becoming identified with successful projects.
Presents case material from Zambian public
bureaucracy. Concludes that while entrepreneurialism is no panacea for development,
it may provide a counterweight to natural
organizational conservatism.

* Dresang, Dennis L. "Ethnic Politics, Representative Bureaucracy, and Development
Administration." Cited as item 199.

483. Dresang, Dennis L. *The Zambia Civil Service:
Entrepreneurialism and Development Adminis-
tration*. Nairobi: East African Publishing
House, 1974.

Discusses the role and performance of the
Zambian bureaucracy in achieving economic
growth and development. Provides political
and administrative history from Northern
Rhodesia period. Argues that bureaucracy
can indeed stimulate development; elaborates
concepts of bureaucratic "entrepreneurialism,"
and provides case illustrations.

* Eldersveld, Samuel J.V. Jagannadham and A.P.
Barnabas. *The Citizen and the Administrator in a Developing Democracy*. Cited as
item 609.

484. Esman, Milton. *Administration and Development
     in Malaysia: Institutions and Reform in a
     Plural Society*. Ithaca: Cornell University
     Press, 1972.

     The fragile political consensus in Malaysia,
     which is riddled with ethnic and linguistic
     cleavages, is held together in large part by
     senior administrative officials. Book de-
     scribes efforts to strengthen training capa-
     bilities of these senior administrators
     through "institution-building." Describes
     context of administration, and some of its
     history; also outlines the values of adminis-
     trators toward the world and other people.
     Most of study devoted to explaining the
     "Montgomery-Esman Report" on administrative
     reform in Malaysia and the course of its
     implementation. Defends an elite-centered
     approach to reform in situations of communal
     conflict.

485. Fabry, Alain. "La Rationalisation dans
     1'Administration Malgache." *International
     Review of Administrative Sciences*, 37, 4
     (1971), 363-377.

     Madagascar has begun to construct a frame-
     work for development administration that will
     allow it to achieve its political objective.
     Steps in this direction have been impeded by
     a too-empirical approach, however, in which
     the government decided on administrative re-
     forms before it determined the general role
     of administration. Computer technology has
     already been put to good use, and a rational-
     ized budget system is about to be installed.
     The success of the latter enterprise will
     depend on a complete reorganization of the
     civil service and more interdepartmental
     coordination.

486. Gable, Richard W. and J. Fred Springer.
     "Administrative Implications of Development
     Policy: A Comparative Analysis of Agricul-
     tural Programs in Asia." *Educational*

Development and Cultural Change, 27, 4
(July 1979), 687-704.

Reports results of a cross-national survey
of 1,815 public officials working in agricultural agencies in Indonesia, Korea, the Philippines and Thailand. Point of analysis is to
determine capacity of agencies to increase
agricultural productivity. Supplemented with
case material and background statistics on
rice production in each country. Concludes
that general "development administration"
solutions are inadequate. Need middle-range
theory to match the diversity of developing
countries.

*   Gamage, Cyril and Martin Minogue. "The District Political Authority System in Sri
  Lanka." Cited as item 568.

487. Gant, George F. *Development Administration:
  Concepts, Goals, Methods*. Madison: University of Wisconsin Press, 1979.

  Comprehensive text on development administration. Treats several specific policy areas
  (agriculture, population, education, public
  enterprise) and administrative processes
  (planning, budgeting, personnel, training).

488. Greenberg, Martin H. *Bureaucracy and Development: A Mexican Case Study*. Lexington,
  Massachusetts: D.C. Heath and Co., 1970.

  Case study of the Mexican Ministry of
  Hydraulic Resources. Mainly interested in
  assessing the efficiency of the organization,
  as a way of responding to theoretical concerns about bureaucracies in transitional
  societies. Data drawn from interviews and
  field observations. Finds relatively high
  level of efficiency and innovation, contrary
  to expectations. This was true despite the
  existence of formalism, personalism, patronage,

and corruption.

489. Grindle, Merilee S. *Bureaucrats, Politicians,
     and Peasants in Mexico: A Case Study in
     Public Policy.* Berkeley: University of
     California Press, 1977.

     Studies the <u>Compañia Nacional de Subsistencía
     Popular</u> (*Conasupo,* or National Staple Products
     Company) as a way to understand the roles of
     bureaucrats and politicians in the Mexican
     policy process. *Conasupo* is responsible for
     buying and selling basic food commodities
     to control supplies and prices. Data drawn
     from interviews with 78 administrators and 19
     non-administrators. Seeks to explain distinc-
     tive (non-Weberian) patterns of Mexican bureau-
     cracy, using in part a patrimonialist frame-
     work.

490. Hamilton, B.L. *Problems of Administration in
     an Emergent Nation: A Case Study of Jamaica.*
     New York: Praeger, 1965.

     Descriptive overview of Jamaican public
     administration. Bulk of study focuses on
     immediate pre-independence period, emphasizing
     themes of preparation for an end to British
     rules. Organized around specific problem
     areas, such as personnel management and the
     survival of British attitudes in the bureau-
     cracy. The concluding chapter adds some infor-
     mation on the immediate post-independence
     period.

491. Hansen, Gary. "Rural Administration and
     Agricultural Development in Indonesia."
     Pacific Affairs, 44, 3 (Fall 1971), 390-
     400.

     Assesses the capacity of the Indonesian
     administrative structure to oversee implementa-
     tion of a rice development plan inaugurated in
     1974. Surveys existing problems in ministerial
     organization. Notes lack of village level

organization. Suggests reducing production
targets until administrative reform can be
undertaken.

492. Honey, John C. *Toward Strategies for Public
Administration Development in Latin America.*
Syracuse: Syracuse University Press, 1968.

First half of book is Honey's analysis of
problems of public administration in Latin
America generally, with his proposals for
strengthening administrative institutions;
second half consists in four critical responses
by specialists in Brazil, Chile, Peru, and
Venezuela.

493. Hope, K.R. "Development Administration in
Post-Independence Guyana." *International
Review of Administrative Sciences,* 43, 1
(1977), 67-72.

Examines the structure of Guyana's development administration, and argues for (1)
enhanced training to root out vestiges of
colonial days; (2) greater decentralization;
(3) accelerated economic development; and (4)
securing the support of the political leadership for administrative reform.

494. Hyden, Goren, Robert Jackson and John Okumu,
eds. *Development Administration: The
Kenyan Experience.* Nairobi: Oxford University Press, 1970.

Fourteen essays dealing with all aspects of
public administration in Kenya. Topics range
from socio-economic environment of administration to the role of co-operatives in rural
development.

495. Ilchman, Warren F. and Norman T. Uphoff. *The
Political Economy of Change.* Berkeley:
University of California Press, 1969.

Analysis of bureaucracy within broader exchange model of politics. Looks at resources,
costs, environments and implications as they
bear on political and administrative decisions.
Although there are scattered references to
specific countries, primarily a general theoretical treatment.

496. Islam, Nasir and Georges M. Henault. "From
      GNP to Basic Needs: A Critical Review of
      Development and Development Administration."
      *International Review of Administrative
      Sciences*, 45, 3 (1979), 253-267.

      Discusses two "models" of development
      administration, which are seen as having
      developed successively in the past thirty
      years. The first is economically oriented,
      tied to industrialization and urbanization.
      The second is rooted in self-reliance, rural
      products, and individual needs. These must
      be seen as ends of a continuum, with the pres-
      ent task to develop a contingency view so as
      to know better when to apply the insights of
      each.

497. Jones, Garth N. "Frontiersmen in Search for
      the 'Lost Horizon': The State of Develop-
      ment Administration in the 60's." *Public
      Administration Review*, 36, 1 (January/
      February 1976), 99-109.

      Book review of Braibanti's *Political and
      Administrative Development*, Riggs's *Frontiers
      of Development Administration*, Waldo's,
      *Temporal Dimensions of Development Administra-
      tion* and Heaphey's *Spatial Dimensions of
      Development Administration*. Jones places these
      in context by analyzing 25 years of American
      technical assistance. Argues that the era of
      collaborative technical assistance for develop-
      ment is past.

498. Kasfir, Nelson. "Development Administration in Africa." *Canadian Journal of African Studies*, 3, 1 (Winter 1969), 99-103.

Focuses on the politics-administration balance in African development administration. Administration in Africa tends to be more politicized than in the developed world, due to the weakness of constituent political institutions and the inability to engage in routine planning. This suggests that any transfer of administrative technology should be undertaken cautiously.

499. Kasfir, Nelson. "Prismatic Theory and African Administration." *World Politics*, 21, 3 (1969), 295-314.

Reviews Riggs' *Administration in Developing Countries* (item 520) and Riggs' *Thailand: The Modernization of a Bureaucratic Polity* (item 525). Analyzes extent to which theory of prismatic society and sala model of bureaucracy, which had been developed using Southeast Asian examples, are applicable to African context. Presents balanced assessment of pros and cons of Riggs' work. Concludes that these works do not provide a theory capable of explaining African administrative behavior, though they do offer an inventory of potentially important factors.

500. Khan, J. "Administrative Change and Development in Barbados." *International Review of Administrative Sciences*, 41, 2 (1975), 149-158.

Describes the evolution of administration in Barbados since independence in 1966. Outlines the structure of the civil service, salary provisions, training opportunities, planning processes and managerial reforms.

501. LaPalombara, Joseph, ed. *Bureaucracy and Political Development*. Princton: Princeton University Press, 1963.

     Thirteen essays on the role of bureaucracy in economic and political modernization. Includes items 53, 77, 521.

502. LaPorte, R. "Administrative, Political, and Social Constraints on Economic Development in Ceylon." *International Review of Administrative Sciences*, 36, 2 (1970), 158-172.

     Although Ceylon's elite prides itself on its British heritage of competitive political democracy, its administrative inheritance has been wholly ineffective in achieving economic development. Indeed, it has presented a serious impediment. Presents a case study of the River Valleys Development Board and maintains that the Ceylonese bureaucracy was riddled with infighting, poor management and fear of risk-taking. Moreover, individual bureaucrats exploited communal tensions for personal gain.

503. Lee, Hahn-Been. "The Role of the Higher Civil Service Under Rapid Social and Political Change." *Development Administration in Asia* (item 551).

     Examines the role of higher civil service in South Korea. Develops a typology of administrative roles based on the time orientations of officials, which is used to discuss their innovation-potential.

504. Leonard, David K. *Reaching the Peasant Farmer: Organization Theory and Practice in Kenya*. Chicago and London: The University of Chicago Press, 1977.

     Presents a case study of the organizational problems of agricultural extension in Kenya, with general prescriptions offered for all developing nations. Applies standard theories of organization and finds them relevant to Kenya. Finds too much central control of local initiatives. At the same time, contrary to the conventional wisdom of development administration, argues for definable performance criteria, formalization, routinization and depersonalization of many decisions.

505. Loveman, Brian. "The Comparative Administration Group, Development Administration, and Antidevelopment." *Public Administration Review*, 36, 6 (November/December 1976), 616-621.

Views CAG as attempt to find a non-Marxist definition of development. "Administrative development" would lessen the chances of communist takeovers in Third World countries, and was thus congruent with U.S. foreign policy. Also led to support for authoritarian and military regimes as "best" administrative developers.

506. Mathur, Kuldeep. "Administrative Mind in a Developing Nation: An Empirical Exploration." *Indian Journal of Public Administration*, 16, 4 (October/December 1970), 575-596.

Assesses the "behavioral orientation" of development bureaucrats in India in an effort to identify their "self-images." Data based on survey of random sample of Block Development Officers in Rajasthan and Uttar Pradesh, with 89 interviews completed. Notes large differences between attitudes in the two provinces. The greater "autocratism" of Rajasthani administrators is attributed to relative lack of exposure to politics and political democracy.

507. Mauzy, Diane K. "Two Rural Development Strategies: Organization, Administrative

Performance and Political Priorities in
India and Malaysia." *Philippine Journal
of Public Administration*, 19, 1-2 (January/
April 1975), 84-112.

Applies Esman's dominant mass party versus
competitive interest-oriented party model
to comparative study of Indian and Malaysian
administrative development strategies. Finds
stronger attachment to integrative values in
Indian case, communal values in Malaysian.

508. Milne, R.S. "Bureaucracy and Development
     Administration." *Public Administration*
     (London), 51 (Winter 1973), 411-426.

Contrary to the case made by many, bureaucracy does not constitute an obstacle to
development. Although some of its features
may need to be modified, it is useful, and
indeed inevitable. Concludes that there are
no easy structural solutions to administrative
problems in poor countries.

509. Milne, R.S. "Mechanistic and Organic Models
     of Public Administration in Developing
     Countries." *Administrative Science Quarter-
     ly*, 15, 1 (March 1970), 57-67.

Discusses Fred Riggs' and Victor Thompson's
views on public administration shortcomings
in developing countries. Notes that Thompson
advocates an organic organizational model
for these nations, in contradistinction to the
mechanistic model usually prescribed and
followed. Argues that neither is appropriate.
Developed countries can make use of both
models, but developing countries cannot follow
either because of their peculiar cultures.
Administration in developing countries can
be improved only by changing their cultures.

510. Montgomery, John D.   "The Populist Front in
     Rural Development: Or Shall We Eliminate
     the Bureaucrats and Get On with the Job?"
     Public Administration Review, 39, 1 (Janu-
     ary/February 1979), 58-65.

     Suggests that an ideology of populism in
     rural development has arisen that takes as
     its central proposition the idea that local
     citizen participation is the key to change.
     The problem is that an attachment to extreme
     localism is just as "debilitating" as over-
     enthusiasm for central, bureaucratically
     directed management.   Local institutions and
     central institutions both need to be strong,
     and to be mutually supportive.

511. Montgomery, John D.   *Technology and Civil
     Life: Making and Implementing Development
     Decisions.*   Cambridge, Massachusetts: The
     MIT Press, 1974.

     Critical examination of traditional
     approaches to underdevelopment.   Argues that
     Western theories have been too oriented toward
     macrodevelopment, national planning, and so
     forth to the detriment of those most in need.
     Technology can play a key role in development,
     but it must be linked to redistributed politi-
     cal power and imaginative administration.

512. Morgan, E. Philip ed.   *The Administration of
     Change in Africa.*   New York: Dunellen, 1974.

     Twelve essays on development administration
     in Africa.   Includes pieces on the theory of
     development administration and the African
     administrative context, as well as several
     case studies.   Contributors include Milton
     Esman, Denis Goulet, Irving Swerdlow and John
     Montgomery, among others.

513. Morgan, E. Philip. "Rural Development Management: Some Lessons From Kenya." *International Review of Administrative Sciences*, 45, 2 (1979), 165-168.

Reviews the impact of the Programming and Implementation Management System (PIM) developed for the Special Rural Development Programme (SRDP) in Kenya in the early 1970's to handle the particular problems of decentralized management. Finds that the system did not have the requisite support of top management.

514. Najjar, George K. "Development Administration and 'New' Public Administration: A Convergence of Perspectives?" *Public Administration Review*, 34, 6 (November/December 1974), 584-587.

Both development administration and the "new" public administration share important assumptions. An explicit synthesis of these two approaches would be an important contribution to public administration.

515. Ness, Gayl D. *Bureaucracy and Rural Development in Malaysia.* Berkeley: Univeristy of California Press, 1967.

Seeks to explain relative success of Malaysia in achieving economic growth in the post-colonial period. Focuses on organizations established to spur development--the Rural and Industrial Development Authority, the Federal Land Development Authority, and community development organizations--and the control exercised over them by politicians. The Ministry of Rural Development in Malaysia, perhaps unusually, used its political power to help achieve effective administrative coordination.

516. Picard, Louis A. "Bureaucrats, Cattle, and
     Public Policy: Land Tenure Changes in
     Botswana." *Comparative Political Studies*,
     13, 3 (October 1980), 313-356.

     As the dominant socioeconomic elites in
     many Third World countries, bureaucrats often
     have a vested interest in the policies they
     formulate and implement. This generalization
     is supported in a study of Botswana's land
     tenure policy process. Bureaucrats stood to
     benefit disproportionately from a shift from
     traditional to freehold tenure, a shift which
     may be counterproductive overall given the
     pressures for increased agricultural and
     grazing land.

517. Picard, Louis A. "Rural Development in
     Botswana: Administrative Structures and
     Public Policy." *Journal of Developing
     Areas*, 13, 3 (April 1979), 283-300.

     Examines rural development policy process
     in Botswana from 1970 to 1974, with emphasis
     on the role of administrative elites. Begins
     with evolution of rural development policy and
     describes in detail the bureaucratic politics
     that brought it into being. Concludes with
     observations on the role of external change
     agents in rural development.

518. Price, Robert. *Society and Bureaucracy in
     Contemporary Ghana*. Berkeley: University of
     California Press, 1975.

     Asks, how can effective organizations be
     created in transitional societies? Focuses on
     the role orientations of Ghanaian civil ser-
     vants and the role expectations of significant
     others, particularly clients. Adopts an
     ecological theoretical perspective, maintain-
     ing that effective organizational behavior is
     a reflection of appropriate supportive rela-
     tionships with the environment. In Ghana,
     the relationships between administrative

organizations and the environment inhibit
the achievement of organizational effectiveness.

519. Quick, Stephen A. "Bureaucracy and Rural
    Socialism in Zambia." *Journal of Modern
    African Studies*, 15, 3 (September 1977),
    379-400.

    Examines Zambian government's involvement
    in encouraging rural cooperative movement.
    Argues that the failure of rural co-operatives
    in Zambia was a product of government action,
    not rural reaction. Suggests five steps that
    might be taken to avoid problem in future: (1)
    administer through mass-based, non-bureaucratic
    organizations; (2) undertake only after
    thorough social analysis; (3) anticipate and
    provide for peasant resistance; (4) be willing
    to make program the only mode of production;
    and (5) commit elite to socialist mode of
    development.

520. Riggs, Fred W. *Administration in Developing
    Countries: The Theory of Prismatic Society.*
    Boston: Houghton Mifflin Co., 1964.

    Primary statement of the Riggs position
    on the comparative study of administration.
    Presents the idea of "prismatic society" to
    explain the dynamics of political and adminis-
    trative development. The prismatic model
    represents a structural-functional, ecological
    approach to comparative analysis that empha-
    sizes environmental influences. The "sala
    model" is the prismatic society's bureaucratic
    expression.

521. Riggs, Fred W. "Bureaucrats and Political
    Development: A Paradoxical View." *Bureau-
    cracy and Political Development* (item 501).

    Improved systems of public administration
    alone in developing countries will not pro-

mote political development; indeed, they may
have the opposite effect. It is critical
that political institutions be strengthened
so as to provide controls over and checks on
bureaucracy.

522. Riggs, Fred W. "The Dialectics of Develop-
     mental Conflict." *Comparative Political
     Studies*, 1, 2 (July 1968), 197-226.

     Students of development have mistakenly
     assumed that political and administrative
     change is irreversible, uni-directional and
     free of conflict. Constructs a "dialectical
     model" of development that is aimed at ex-
     plaining conflict resolution and institutional-
     ization.

523. Riggs, Fred W., ed. *Frontiers of Development
     Administration*. Durham: Duke University
     Press, 1971.

     Nineteen essays sponsored by the Comparative
     Administration Group. Some are broadly con-
     ceptual, others deal with specific areas, such
     as China, Eastern Europe, and Africa.

524. Riggs, Fred W. *Prismatic Society Revisited*.
     Morristown, N.J.: General Learning Press,
     1973.

     Clarification and elaboration of the prismat-
     ic model. Discusses dilemmas of power,
     dilemmas of structure and dilemmas of belief
     in prismatic systems.

525. Riggs, Fred W. *Thailand: The Modernization
     of a Bureaucratic Polity*. Honolulu: East-
     West Center Press, 1966.

     Case study of political and administrative
     change in Thailand. Includes both straight
     historical analysis and social scientific

speculation. Basic argument is that Thailand represents a "bureaucratic polity," which is a political system with weak political institutions unable to exercise effective control of administration. Although this system is reasonably stable, it is incapable of modernizing.

526. Rondinelli, D.A. and K. Ruddle. "Local Organizations for Integrated Rural Development: Implementing Equity Policy in Developing Countries." *International Review of Administrative Sciences*, 43, 1 (1977), 20-30.

Surveys experiences with integrated rural development and identifies administrative requirements for effective programs. Two most important administrative preconditions are organizational capability and local government support.

527. Rweyemamu, Anthony H. and Goran Hyden, eds. *A Decade of Public Administration in Africa.* Nairobi: East African Literature Bureau, 1975.

More than twenty articles, mainly by practitioners, on a wide range of subjects concerning African administration. Issues include: Africanization of the public service, development administration, role of civil service versus other governmental actors, and policy-making processes. Articles drawn from papers and discussions at a series of twelve Inter-African Public Administration Seminars.

528. Samoff, Joel. "The Bureaucracy and the Bourgeoisie: Decentralization and Class Structure in Tanzania." *Comparative Studies in Society and History*, 21, 1 (January 1979), 30-62.

Recent research indicates that various institutional reforms in Tanzania designed to

foster increased citizen participation in
development planning may have actually had
the opposite effect; moreover, there has been
no positive impact on rural production. The
reason for this is the continuing domination
of a technocratic ideology, which stems from
the nature of the class struggle in Tanzania.
Since the governing class in Tanzania is
bureaucratic, it is unlikely that the bureaucracy will undertake programs that will open
the gates to its opponents.

529. Schaffer, Bernard B. "Administrative Legacies
and Links in the Post-Colonial State."
Development and Change, 9, 2 (April 1978),
175-200.

Examines continuing links between administrative practices in Anglophonic Africa and
Western theory. The legacy of linkage has
gone through three phases: preparation for
self-government; institutional training for
new public services; and major administrative
reform. The net result has been a strengthening of bureaucratic elitism.

530. Schaffer, Bernard, ed. *Administrative Training and Development*. New York: Praeger,
1974.

Eight essays focused on problems of
administrative training in East Africa, Zambia,
India, and Pakistan. Except for analytical
introduction and conclusion by editor, area-
focused. Includes items 257 and 543.

531. Schaffer, Bernard B. and Huang Wen-hsien.
"Distribution and The Theory of Access."
Development and Change, 6, 2 (April 1975),
13-36.

Discusses the problems of designing governmental services, especially in developing
countries, with clients in mind. Lead article

in special issue on access to public services.
Argues that research on access must be central
to policy planning and program design.

532. Schumacher, Edward J. *Politics, Bureaucracy
     and Rural Development in Senegal.* Berkeley:
     University of California Press, 1975.

     Case study of "institutional change" in
     Senegal's first ten years of independence.
     Applies a standard systems model of the policy
     process as an analytical framework. Finds that
     initial Senegalese plans for social develop-
     ment, which were overly ambitious in scope,
     have been substantially attentuated. Does not
     support the notion that bureaucratic hegemony
     is inevitable. Indeed, Senegal's machine-
     style clientelist politics have inhibited the
     formation of a coherent bureaucracy.

533. Scott, Robert E. "The Government Bureaucrat
     and Political Change in Latin America."
     Journal of International Affairs, 20, 2
     (1966), 289-308.

     Bureaucrats are centrally involved in the
     tasks of modernization in all Latin American
     countries. However, most members of the elite
     civil service ranks feel a primary commitment
     to the maintenance of law and order, with only
     a secondary commitment to change--unlike their
     counterparts in Africa and Asia. Ultimately,
     no group, including the bureaucracy, can
     undertake the taks of modernization without
     help from other sectors of the polity.

534. Seitz, John L. "The Failure of U.S. Technical
     Assistance in Public Administration: The
     Iranian Case." *Public Administration Review,*
     40, 5 (September/October 1980), 407-412.

     Examines two major U.S. public administra-
     tion assistance projects in Iran in the 1953-
     1968 period: aid to Iranian ministeries and

aid to the Iranian police. Not only did they fail to accomplish their objectives, but they contributed to the upheavals of 1978-79. The main reasons for the failure were American ignorance of Iran and anti-communist political objectives.

535. Shuster, James R. "Bureaucratic Transition in Morocco." *Human Organization*, 24, 1 (1965), 53-58.

Treats three main aspects of bureaucracy and development in Morocco: (1) the centrality of administration as a developmental instrument; (2) the problems of "Moroccanization" in recruitment; and (3) the implications of changes in the structure of personnel of the bureaucracy for the future of Moroccan administration. Concludes by saying that the Moroccan bureaucracy has acted responsibly in directing the country toward modernization.

536. Siffin, William J. *The Thai Bureaucracy: Institutional Change and Development.* Honolulu: East-West Center Press, 1966.

Focuses on the historical evolution and structural characteristics of the Thai bureaucracy. Finds enormous continuity through early 1960's, at which time new forces for change--particularly demographic--began building. Follows a generally ecological model, though not heavily theoretical in orientation.

537. Siffin, William J. "Two Decades of Public Administration in Developing Countries." *Public Administration Review*, 36, 1 (January/February 1976), 61-71.

Reviews contributions of American public administration to development processes over the 1955-75 period. Suggests that major hindrance to knowledge transfer was difficulty breaking away from "system maintenance" con-

cepts to developmentally oriented ideas. Positive contributions cited in area of specific
administrative technologies (finance and budgeting).

538. Sigelman, Lee. "Bureaucratic Development and
     Dominance: A New Test of the Imbalance
     Thesis." *Western Political Quarterly*, 27,
     2 (June 1974), 308-313.

     Assesses Riggs' 'imbalance' thesis by test-
     ing the hypothesis that level of bureaucratic
     development and extent of bureaucratic domi-
     nance are positively related. In a sample of
     57 developing nations, finds a high negative
     correlation. Bureaucracies that are highly
     developed do not necessarily dominate Third
     World polities.

539. Spencer, Chuku-Dinka R. "Politics, Public
     Administration and Agricultural Develop-
     ment: A Case Study of the Sierra Leone
     Industrial Plantation Development Program."
     Journal of Developing Areas, 12, 1 (October
     1977), 69-86.

     Analyzes a major unsuccessful agricultural
     development program in Sierra Leone. After
     discussing the background of the project,
     suggests that it failed for a combination of
     administrative, financial and political rea-
     sons. Includes detailed statistics.

540. Sperber, K.W. van. *Public Administration in
     Tanzania*. Munich: Weltforum Verlag, 1970.

     General overview of Tanzanian public
     administration. Heavy emphasis on administra-
     tive patterns under German and British rule.
     Describes post-colonial administrative system
     in broad outline. Includes discussion of
     party-administrative relations, parastatals,
     and Africanization.

541. Springer, J. Fred. "Observation and Theory
     in Development Administration." Adminis-
     tration and Society, 9, 1 (May 1977), 13-
     44.

     Sound empirical theory has not been forth-
     coming in comparative administration mainly
     because scholars have either (1) analyzed too
     many variables in too few cases or (2) ana-
     lyzed too few variables in too many cases.
     Argues for middle range, organizational level
     comparisons, focusing on factors that are
     potentially amenable to change.

542. Stahl, O. Glenn. "Managerial Effectiveness
     in Developing Countries." International
     Review of Administrative Sciences, 45, 1
     (1979), 1-5.

     Brief and self-consciously impressionistic
     review of the present causes of administrative
     effectiveness in developing countries, with a
     stress on cultural impediments. Argues that
     fundamental changes in habits and attitudes
     must precede effective and efficient manage-
     ment.

543. Stamp, Patricia. "The East African Staff
     College." Administrative Training and
     Development (item 530).

     Compares the East African Staff College with
     the Kenyan Institute of Administration. Notes
     lower level of institutionalization of former,
     a function of its status as a regional organi-
     zation.

544. Strauss, Bertram W. "Malawi's Path as an
     Emerging Nation." Public Administration
     Review, 24, 3 (September 1964), 166-169.

     Malawi's transition to independence was
     less chaotic and disruptive than usual because
     political and administrative measures were

carefully prepared in advance.

545. Swerdlow, Irving ed. *Development Administra-*
     tion. Syracuse: Syracuse University Press,
     1963.

     Eight essays plus an introduction by the
     editor. Contributors include Merle Fainsod,
     Lucian Pye and Albert Waterston, among others.
     Emphasizes general theoretical issues (plan-
     ning, politics, organization, etc.) rather
     than specific case studies.

546. Taub, Richard P. *Bureaucrats Under Stress:*
     Administrators and Administration in an
     Indian State. Berkeley: University of
     California, 1969.

     Empirical study of a group of senior civil
     servants in the small Indian capital city of
     Bhubaneswar in Orissa state. Seeks to explore
     the potential of bureaucracies in democratic
     nations to achieve their developmental goals.
     "Stress" comes from the difficulty of reach-
     ing these goals and from tensions with other
     actors. Draws on Weber for analytical in-
     sights. Concludes that the bureaucratic model
     is inappropriate in developmental contexts.

547. Thompson, Victor A. "Administrative Objectives
     for Development Administration." *Adminis-*
     trative Science Quarterly, 9, 1 (June 1964),
     91-108.

     Western administrative practices are general-
     ly control-oriented. They are thus ill-suited
     for administration in developing countries
     where adaptability and change are needed above
     all. Some adaptive principles can be derived
     from behavioral science research, however.
     Concern with innovation, goal-sharing, com-
     bining planning and doing, minimizing parochi-
     alism, diffusing influence, increasing inde-
     pendence and avoiding bureaupathology are
     among the objectives of modern behavioral

science that can be transferred to the
developing world.

548. Tilman, Robert O. *Bureaucratic Transition
in Malaya.* Durham: Duke University Press,
1964.

Although formidable problems face bureaucracies in developing countries, Malaya has
managed to surmount most of them. It has
successfully imported a modern administrative
structure, replaced foreign officials with
indigenous employees, and maintained a high
level of organizational effectiveness.

549. Timsit, Gérard. "Fonction Publique et
Developpement Politique: Le Cas des stats
Africaines Francophones." *International
Review of Administrative Sciences,* 38, 1
(1972), 1-11.

Argues that the colonial administrative
legacy in francophone Africa has been neither
wholly integrative nor wholly disintegrative.
While the legacy of intermingled political
and administrative powers has generally been
integrative, it has also provided for a dual
hierarchy that permits frequent conflict.
Scattered references are made to Algeria,
Gabon, Guinea, Burundi, Mauritania, Upper
Volta, Madagascar, and Zaire.

550. Van Nieuwenhujze, C.A.O. "Public Administration, Comparative Administration, Development Administration: Concepts and Theory in
their Struggle for Relevance." *Development
and Change,* 5, 3 (1973-74), 1-18.

Focuses on the general relevance of public
administration theory. Traces different under-
standings of public administration in North
America, Europe, and the developing world.

* Waldo, Dwight. "Comparative and Development Administration: Retrospect and Prospect." Cited as item 33.

* Warnapala, W.A. "District Agencies of Government Departments in Ceylon." Cited as item 602.

551. Weidner, Edward W. ed. *Development Administration in Asia*. Durham: Duke University Press, 1970.

   Thirteen essays on various aspects of Asian development administration. Country studies of Korea, the Philippines, Japan, India, Pakistan, and Vietnam. Includes item 503.

552. Whyte, William F. "Imitation or Innovation: Reflections on the Institutional Development of Peru." *Administrative Science Quarterly*, 13, 3 (December 1968), 370-385.

   Argues that imitation of administrative models from industrialized countries is dysfunctional for developing nations, which have distinct cultures and needs. The best strategy for developing nations is innovation, with an emphasis on integrating existing local specialties and resources. Case material from Peru is used to illustrate the argument.

553. Ziring, Lawrence and Robert LaPorte, Jr. "The Pakistan Bureaucracy: Two Views." *Asian Survey*, 14, 12 (December 1974), 1086-1104.

   Discusses administrative reforms of Ali Bhutto in the post-1972 period. Provoked by traditional bureaucratic hegemony vis-à-vis civilian politicians, the elite Civil Service of Pakistan has been ended and merged with the All-Pakistan Unified Grades. It is not yet clear whether a "new bureaucratic order" will emerge, nor whether these structural reforms will further regime developmental goals.

CHAPTER 9

LOCAL AND FIELD ADMINISTRATION

This chapter consists mainly of references to books and articles about administrative questions in cities, towns, and other subnational units of government. Also included are citations of works that deal with central or national administrative presence in local areas; this is the meaning of the term "field administration."

554. Abedin, Najmul. *Local Administration and Politics in Modernizing Societies: Bangladesh and Pakistan*. London: Oxford University Press, 1978.

Historical treatment of the evolution of local administration in Bangladesh (and Pakistan) from 1947 to 1973. Describes the structure of district administration, bureaucratic attitudes toward development and the functions of local administration. Also treats the changing relationship between politics and administration.

* Allinson, Gary D. "Public Servants and Public Interests in Contemporary Japan." Cited as item 153.

* Aquino, Belinda A. "Dimensions of Development in Philippine Provinces, 1970." Cited as item 473.

555. Ashford, Douglas. "Resources, Spending and
     Party Politics in British Local Govern-
     ment." *Administration and Society*, 7, 3
     (November 1975), 286-311.

     Assesses the influence of political parti-
     sanship on patterns of local government
     spending in Britain. Despite ideological
     differences on how spending should be related
     to local resource bases between Labour and
     Conservative parties, no differences in fact
     are found.

556. Barnes, Samuel H. "Decision-Making in
     Italian Local Politics: The View of the
     Communal Councilor." *Administration and
     Society*, 6, 2 (August 1974), 179-204.

     Analyzes the extent to which local Italian
     politics is (a) dominated by the mayor,
     interest groups, or parties; (b) democratic
     or undemocratic; and (c) dependent on bureau-
     crats or outside experts. Data drawn from
     interviews with 382 communal councilors.
     Finds that patterns of local decisional
     processes vary greatly depending on region,
     although mayor is stong everywhere.

557. Bassanini, F. "L'Experience de la Regionali-
     sation en Italie." *International Review of
     Administrative Sciences*, 43, 1 (1977), 51-
     61.

     Reviews the fitful history of administrative
     regionalism in Italy since the 19th century.
     Concludes that the success of recent efforts,
     such as the 1975 Regions Act and the 1976
     Regional Accounts Act, cannot yet be evaluated.

558. Baum, Edward. "Recent Administrative Reform
     in Local Government in Northern Nigeria."
     Journal of Developing Areas, 7, 1 (October
     1972), 75-88.

Suggests that the Federal military government worked a "quiet revolution" in Northern
Nigerian administrative structures. Traditional rulers lost considerable political
power as new states were created and the old
"national authorities" abolished. Furthermore, considerable decentralization and
democratization in governmental power has
taken place.

559. Bonnaud-Delamare, Roger. "Le Préfet dans le
     Cadre de la Constitution Française de
     1958." *International Review of Administra-*
     tive Sciences, 27, 1 (1961), 5-15.

     Discusses changes in the power and status
     of French prefects under the Gaullist consti-
     tution. Most changes have been minor. Pre-
     fects can be retired earlier and transferred
     more easily. Some prefectoral power--in law
     and order and economics--has been enhanced,
     though their authority over small communes
     has been decreased. In general, there has
     been an effort to make the prefect a more
     pliant instrument of government policy.

560. Brickman, Ronald. "Patterns of Administrative
     Decentralization in France." *Administration*
     and Society, 11, 3 (November 1979), 283-
     306.

     Analyzes the extent and impact of administra-
     tive decentralization in French higher educa-
     tion following the 1968 demonstrations. Case
     illustrates why French decentralization efforts
     usually fail--and how they might succeed.
     Local autonomy did increase in universities,
     although the reasons why may be peculiar to
     this domain.

561. Cheema, G. Shabbir. "Changing Patterns of
     Administration in the Field: The Malaysian
     Case." *International Review of Administra-*
     tive Sciences, 45, 1 (1979), 64-68.

Despite article's title, argues that field
structure established in colonial period has
remained relatively intact, with an important
role for the district officer as chief representative of the national bureaucracy.

562. Cole, Taylor. *The Canadian Bureaucracy and
Federalism*. Denver: Graduate School of
International Studies, 1966.

Brief appraisal of post-war developments in
Canadian public administration. Focuses
primarily on implications of these developments for Canadian federalism, particularly
the Quebec question. Reviews various Royal
Commissions (including Glassco) and the
operation of "control agencies" such as the
Treasury Board and the Civil Service Commission.

*   Cowart, Andrew T. "Partisan Politics and
the Budgetary Process in Oslo." Cited as
item 410.

*   Cowart, Andrew T., Tore Hansen and Karl-Erik
Brofoss. "Budgetary Strategies and Success
at Multiple Decision Levels in the Norwegian Urban Setting." Cited as item 411.

*   Crozier, Michel and Jean-Claude Thoenig. "The
Regulation of Complex Organizational Systems." Cited as item 348.

563. Fesler, James W. "The Political Role of
Field Administration." *Papers in Comparative Public Administration* (item 9).

The field administrative system tends to
take on a more powerful political role in
those societies lacking consensus and stability.
Maintenance of law and order is concentrated
in the hands of a single territorial repre-

sentative of the national government.

564. Fried, Robert C. "Communism, Urban Budgets
     and the Two Italies." *Journal of Politics*,
     33, 4 (November 1971), 1008-1051.

     Analyzes budgets of 31 Italian cities in an
     effort to weigh the importance of partisan
     politics in Italian municipal government.
     Finds that party is not the most important
     variable, though it sometimes has an impact.
     Also finds that the direction of party in-
     fluence is not always consistent with party
     ideology.

565. Fried, Robert C. *The Italian Prefects:* A
     Study in Administrative Politics. New
     Haven: Yale University Press, 1963.

     Focuses on the role of prefects in Italian
     field administration, though sets in context
     of Italian politics in general. Presents
     historically, covering period from pre-19th
     century through the post-World War II years.
     Concludes by presenting a set of propositions
     specific to the Italian prefectoral system and
     a set intended to apply to prefectoral sys-
     tems generally. Systematically describes
     the differences between prefectoral and
     functional field systems, as well as between
     integrated and unintegrated prefectoral sys-
     tems; the French and Italian, respectively,
     correspond to these latter two types.

566. Fritz, Dan. "The Dynamics of Political-
     Administrative Relations in Rural India: A
     Case Study in Mysore." *Asian Profile*, 3,
     5 (October 1975), 461-475.

     Analyzes the day-to-day operations of the
     Panchayati Raj program in Mysore state.
     Identifies problems that structure local-
     level political and administrative relations.
     Present perceptions of program from per-

spectives of various actors, including villagers, politicians and administrators.

567. Frojd, A. "Municipal Self-Government and
     Regional Development in Sweden." *Inter-
     national Review of Administrative Sciences*,
     36, 3 (1970), 251-255.

     Generally describes Swedish local govern-
     ment, with an emphasis on administrative re-
     forms in the 1960's. Notes the important
     role of Swedish municipalities in economic
     development and regional planning, though
     stresses the fact that they are viewed as
     mainly instrumental and that the government
     will amalgamate and consolidate units when
     necessary to rationalize structures.

568. Gamage, Cyril and Martin Minogue. "The Dis-
     trict Political Authority System in Sri
     Lanka." *Journal of Administration Overseas*,
     17, 4 (October 1978), 270-281.

     Discusses a case study of "developmental
     engineering" in Sri Lanka that revolved around
     the establishment of a "district political
     authority system." The purpose of this sys-
     tem was to address some of the central
     dilemnas of development administration by
     avoiding bureaucratic centralization through
     the assertion of control by local elected
     political representatives. Concludes that
     this reform was reasonably successful.

569. Gertzel, Cherry. "The Provincial Administra-
     tion in Kenya." *Journal of Commonwealth
     Political Studies*, 4, 3 (September 1965),
     201-215.

     Describes post-independence Kenyan Govern-
     ment's use of the provincial administration
     to extend central control over the country-
     side. This parallels its functions during
     the colonial period.

570. Graham, Lawrence. "Centralization versus
     Decentralization Dilemmas in the Administra-
     tion of Public Service." *International Re-
     view of Administrative Sciences*, 46, 3 (1980),
     219-232.

     After discussing three models of administra-
     tive field structures--the prefect-governor,
     the socialist prefectural, and the local
     autonomy systems--argues that our lack of
     knowledge about the proper mix of centraliza-
     tion and decentralization can be rectified
     by neither more narrow gauge studies aimed at
     producing program reorganizations or broad
     academic theories pitched at the level of
     whole administrative structures. Instead, we
     need research that comprehends the nexus of
     intergovernmental relations in specific policy
     areas.

571. Greenwood, Royston. "Relations Between Central
     and Local Government in Sweden: The Control
     of Local Government Expenditure." *Public
     Administration* (London), 57, (Winter 1979),
     457-470.

     Problems in the Swedish economy, triggered
     by the rise in oil prices in the early 1970's,
     led to an attempted expansion of central
     government control over local expenditures.
     Unlike Britain, however, where central control
     is effective, the Swedish effort proved un-
     successful. Based on interviews with local
     officials, concludes that the major reason
     for this lack of success is a deeply ingrained
     cultural norm that local authorities should
     be independent and should exercise sole con-
     trol over local income taxes.

*   Greenwood, Royston, C.R. Hinings and Stewart
     Ranson. "The Politics of the Budgetary
     Process in English Local Government." Cited
     as item 423.

*   Greenwood, Royston, C.R. Hinings and Stewart
      Ranson. "Contingency Theory and the
      Organization of Local Authorities: Part I:
      Differentiation and Integration." Cited as
      item 359.

*   Hinings, C.R., Royston Greenwood and Stewart
      Ranson. "Contingency Theory and the
      Organization of Local Authorities: Part II:
      Contingencies and Structure." Cited as
      item 362.

572. Hough, Jerry F. *The Soviet Prefects: The
      Local Party Organs in Industrial Decision-
      Making.* Cambridge, Massachusetts: Harvard
      University Press, 1969.

      Analyzes the economic activities of the
      regional Communist Party apparatus in the
      Soviet Union. Based on reading of regional
      press, biographical sources, and some inter-
      views. Tries to elucidate "Soviet administra-
      tive theory" and principles of management.
      Suggests that the prefectural systems of
      Western Europe are the best guide in under-
      standing Soviet administrative behavior, since
      regional officials have comparable political
      authority.

573. Jacob, Herbert. *German Administration Since
      Bismarck: Central Authority Versus Local
      Autonomy.* New Haven: Yale University Press,
      1963.

      Major historical study of German field
      administration since 1870. Central question
      is how a national government can impose its
      will over a large territorial state. Ques-
      tion is addressed by focusing on the idea of
      "responsiveness," which is defined as the
      compliance of field agents with central
      directives. Notes that for most of the time
      since 1870, German central government has not
      used its own field agents, but has instead

relied on state government apparatus. Concludes with the observation that German
administration has, overall, been stable,
effective and responsive.

574. Krannich, Ronald L. "The Politics of Intergovernmental Relations in Thailand."
Asian Survey, 19, 5 (May 1979), 506-522.

Examines linkages between central Thai
government and 118 municipal governmental
units. Uses intergovernmental term here
within a unitary, not a federal, framework.
The key dynamic of Thai intergovernmental
relations is "continuous central administrative levelling of local political processes."

575. Kuper, Adam and Simon Gillett. "Aspects of
Administration in Western Botswana."
African Studies, 29, 3 (1970), 169-182.

Analyzes the relationship between African
villagers and district government in the
Kalahari region of Botswana. Provides background information on geography, ethnography,
and economy of region. Treats pre- and post-
independence periods. Concludes that district
commissioners continue to exercise paramount
roles.

576. Letowski, J. "Les Reformes de l'Administra-
tion Locale en Pologne de 1972 à 1975."
*International Review of Administrative
Sciences*, 42, 1 (1976), 23-32.

In the period 1972 to 1975, three major
stages of local government reform took place
in Poland, rationalizing the size of the
units and their relationship to other units
of government.

577. Lischeron, Joe and Toby D. Wall. "Attitudes
Towards Participation Among Local Authority

Employees." *Human Relations*, 28, 6 (1975), 499-517.

Reports results of survey of 127 blue collar employees in English local government. Finds that while employees experience little actual job participation, they express strong desire to be involved in decision-making. Further notes that attitudes towards participation are positively related to job satisfaction.

578. Ma, Laurence J.C. "The Chinese Approach to City Planning: Policy, Administration and Action." *Asian Survey*, 19, 9 (September 1979), 838-855.

Discusses the city planning policies of the People's Republic of China. Focuses on urban land use, transportation, functional zoning and housing development. Concludes with observations on Chinese efforts to focus attention on spatial needs of small to medium-sized cities.

579. Machin, Howard. *The Prefect in French Public Administration*. London: Croom Helm, 1977.

Analyzes the role of the French prefects in the Fifth Republic. Begins with historical background on evolution of system and discusses the current state of French local government. After examining several recent attempted reforms, including regionalization, and their lack of effect on the prefects, treats relationships between prefects and significant others. Concludes that prefects continue to exercise real power, especially collectively; actual influence varies with the individual relationship prefects develop in local political systems.

580. Milch, Jerome. "Urban Government in France." *Administration and Society*, 9, 4 (February

1978), 467-494.

Relatively little attention is paid to
French local government, since most scholars
assume that administrative centralization
renders it insignificant. This is not
necessarily the case. Presents case analysis
of water resource programs in Montpelier and
Nimes, two southern communes. Despite considerable central pressure, local officials
have managed to formulate projects that
reflect local interests.

581. Miller, J.V. "The Layfield Committee--How
      Would the Implementation of its Recommenda-
      tions Affect Local Government Administra-
      tion." *Public Administration* (London), 55
      (Spring 1977), 17-26.

Reviews the report of the Layfield Committee
on local government expenditure control.
Notes overall centralizing tendencies of the
recommendations, and analyzes various specific
suggestions, such as local income taxes, fee
structures, performance reviews of local
authorities, and audits.

582. Moya, Palencia, Mario. "Federalism and
      Administrative Decentralization." *Inter-
      national Review of Administrative Sciences*,
      40, 1 (1974), 15-22.

Quasi-academic analysis of federal-state
relations in Mexico by the Minister of the
Interior. Includes a history of Mexican
federalism.

583. Neunreither, Karlheinz. "Federalism and West
      Germany Bureaucracy." *Political Studies*,
      7, 3 (October 1959), 233-245.

German federalism is unique in the extent
to which the federal government must rely on
state (Land) administrations to act in areas

reserved for federal policy-making. A mediating element is the Bundesrat, the second
parliamentary chamber, which represents the
states' interests. The situation has led to
close national-state cooperation in legislative planning.

584. Oamar, Felipe V. and Patria Rivera. "Local
Government Developments." *Philippine Jour-
nal of Public Administration,* 19, 1-2
(January/April 1975), 1-14.

Reviews developments in Philippine local
government since the Decentralization Act of
1967. This act, which empowered local chief
executives to appoint and pay subordinate
local officials out of local funds, was reinforced by provisions in the Philippine Con-
stitution of 1973. Shifts to recentralize
began with the martial law proclamation of
1972 and have been heightened since.

585. Park, Yung H. "The Local Public Personnel
System in Japan." *Asian Survey,* 18, 6
(June 1978), 592-608.

Focuses on contemporary Japanese prefectual
personnel system. Central question is the
extent to which the democratization sought
under the Occupation government has been
realized. These post-war reforms were in-
congruent with local culture and traditional
practices, and thus have been incompletely
realized. However, the formal separation of
the local public service system from the
national system, as provided by the Local
Autonomy Law, has contributed to decentralization and pluralization.

586. Picard, Louis A. "Socialism and the Field
Administrator: Decentralization in Tanzania."
Comparative Politics, 12, 4 (July 1980),
439-458.

Tanzania is unique among former British colonies in its attempt to refashion the colonial district administrative structure into an agent of socialist economic change, while at the same time decentralizing the decision-making process. After reviewing some of the reasons this pattern was chosen, concludes that while some deconcentration of power to the regional and district levels has occurred, political decentralization, involving local people in decision-making, has been less successful.

587. Pontier, Jean-Marie. "La Réforme des Collectivitiés Locales en France." *International Review of Administrative Sciences*, 46, 2 (1980), 179-192.

Analyzes the philosophical, political and administrative implications of local government reform as it was being considered by the French parliament in 1978 and 1979.

588. Pusić Eugen. "Territorial and Functional Administration in Yugoslavia." *Administrative Science Quarterly*, 14, 1 (March 1969), 62-72.

Distinguishes two models of administration: territorial and functional. The former is characterized by centralized patterns of decisions with a high dependence on outside political power; the latter by decisions based on technical and professional norms. Using these two models, an empirical analysis of administration in the communes and service institutions of the Zagreb area of Yugoslavia is presented. Concludes that decisional processes there continue to approximate the territorial form.

589. Rees, I.B. "Local Government in Switzerland." *Public Administration* (London), 47 (Winter 1969), 421-450.

Compares Swiss and English systems of local
government administration. Describes canton
and commune system, and includes data on
population size and expenditures. Concludes
that despite decentralization and diversity,
Swiss local government is far healthier than
English. In part, this is due to widespread
political participation and identification with
small units of government.

590. Rezazadeh, Reza. "Local Administration in
    Colombia." *Journal of Administration Over-
    seas*, 9, 2 (April 1970), 110-120.

    Descriptive overview of Colombian local
    governmental structures. Defines functions
    of major institutions at state and local
    levels. Discusses municipal tax administra-
    tion and planning responsibilities.

*   Richardson, Ivan L. "Municipal Government
    in Brazil: The Financial Dimension." Cited
    as item 456.

591. Richardson, Nicholas J. *The French Prefector-
    al Corps*. Cambridge: Cambridge University
    Press, 1966.

    Study of the French prefectoral corps during
    the Restoration, 1814-1830. Focuses on
    recruitment, careers, and corps organization.
    Concluding chapter on the relationship between
    the nobility and the prefectoral corps notes
    high proportion of nobles named to corps by
    Bourbons.

592. Ridley, F.F. "The French Prefectoral System
    Revived." *Administration and Society*, 6, 1
    (May 1974), 48-72.

    Reviews reforms of the prefectoral corps
    during the French Fifth Republic. The prefect
    is now (1974) stronger than ever--the "real

boss" in local areas. Although ministries retain separate ties to local functionaries, field operations are more integrated.

593. Ridley, F.F. "Integrated Decentralization: Models of the Prefectoral System." *Political Studies*, 21, 1 (March 1973), 13-25.

Analyzes the French prefectoral system as a way of understanding means of decentralizing governmental decision-making. Begins with discussion of the roles of the French prefect expressed in English terms--County Manager, Lord Lieutenant, etc.--then outlines various ways in which prefectoral systems can be structured.

594. Sekulić, Ljubo. "Role and Status of Republic Administrative Bodies in Yugoslavia." *International Review of Administrative Sciences*, 42, 2 (1976), 153-160.

Describes the structure and authority of administrative agencies at the level of the Republic in Yugoslavia, in contradistinction to those at local and federal levels.

595. Silberman, Bernard S. "The Role of Prefectural Governors in Japanese Bureaucratic Developments." *Development Administration in Asia* (item 551).

Analyzes the recruitment and tenure of Japanese prefectural officials from 1868 to 1899 and from 1900 to 1945. Concludes that Japanese civil bureaucracy during this time was achievement-oriented, even though some officials continued to be drawn from samurai class.

596. Simpas, Santiago S. "The Role of Local Elites: The Philippine Experience." *Philippine Journal of Public Administration,* 19, 1-2 (January/April 1975), 63-83.

Applies role analysis to provincial and municipal Philippine elites. Finds high degree of orientation toward political and social roles, with only moderate concern for economic, administrative and civic roles.

597. Smith, B.C. "Field Administration and Political Change: The Case of Northern Nigeria." *Administrative Science Quarterly,* 17, 1 (March 1972), 99-109.

Examines role of district officer in Northern Nigeria in colonial and post-colonial periods. Main focus is relationship of field administration to political change. Suggests that district officers play important stabilizing role, though the nature of field administration is dependent on the overall political context.

598. Smith, Brian. "The Measurement of Decentralization." *International Review of Administrative Sciences,* 45, 3 (1979), 214-222.

Treats decentralization as a variable, and discusses ways to conceptualize and measure it, including, among others, taxation, field administration, expenditure, and personnel.

599. Sternheimer, Stephen. "Modernizing Administrative Elites: The Making of Managers for Soviet Cities." *Comparative Politics,* 11, 4 (July 1979), 403-424.

Explores the character of Soviet city managers in an effort to determine extent to which they conform to our preconception of an authoritarian, centralized, party-dominated regime. Constructs statistical profiles for various sized cities. Finds evidence for

nonuniform elite transformation in the USSR,
lending credence to the view that questions
the utility of "partocracy" models. At the
same time, urban administrators who are dis-
posed toward centralism, hierarchy and
mechanistic problem-solving are most highly
rewarded.

600. Taras, Ray. "Democratic Centralism and
Polish Local Government Reforms." *Public
Administration* (London), 53 (Winter 1975),
403-426.

Reviews changes in Polish local government
in the post-war period in the context of the
Leninist concept of democratic centralism,
which has been applied in this area as in party affairs. Includes detailed historical
analysis, as well as some quantitative budget
data. Concludes with a look at the period
of reforms following the overthrow of Gomulka
in 1970.

601. Wagener, Frido. "The Joint Municipal Association for the Rationalization of Organization
and Management in the Federal Republic of
Germany." *Public Administration* (London),
52 (Autumn 1974), 335-349.

Describes the structure and responsibilities
of the Joint Municipal Association for the
Rationalization of Organization and Management, an association of West German local
governments founded in 1947 that is devoted
to solving common problems. The organization
has had a "substantial influence" on the
practice of local government in the Federal
Republic.

602. Warnapala, W.A. "District Agencies of
Government Departments in Ceylon." *International Review of Administrative Sciences*,
38, 2 (1972), 133-140.

Discusses the effect on local administration of extending central government departments to the district level in Ceylon. At first the powers of the territorial officers were diluted, and problems of coordination arose. These have now been ameliorated by the creation of coordinating committees.

603. Zarić, Ljubisa. "Communal Administrative Agencies in Yugoslavia." *International Review of Administrative Sciences*, 42, 2 (1976), 161-166.

Discusses the powers and responsibilities of administrative agencies in Yugoslav communes, which are, in theory, the "basic socio-political community."

CHAPTER 10

CITIZENS AND ADMINISTRATION

This chapter contains references to works pertaining to the relationships between bureaucrats and their clients or the public at large. Reflected in this chapter is the considerable attention paid by scholars of comparative administration to institutions that mediate citizen-bureaucrat interactions, particularly that of the ombudsman.

604. Boim, Leon. "'Ombudsmanship' in the Soviet Union." *American Journal of Comparative Law*, 22, 3 (Summer 1974), 509-540.

Describes the nature and function of the Prokuratura, which is the state organ vested with ultimate control over the processing of citizen complaints and grievances against government. Also describes other complaint-processing mechanisms and institutions, including the press and party structures. Provides some case histories of grievances and their handling.

605. Chapuisat, L.J. "La Médiateur Français on l'Ombudsman Sacrifié." *International Review of Administrative Sciences*, 40, 2 (1974), 109-129.

The French version of the ombudsman, called the Mediator of Administration, has a far narrower competence than its Scandinavian counterpart. One of the chief problems is that citizen complaints do not go directly to the Mediator, but must instead be channeled there by a member of Parliament.

606. Danet, Brenda. "The Language of Persuasion in Bureaucracy: 'Modern' and 'Traditional' Appeals to the Israeli Customs Authorities." *American Sociological Review*, 36, 5 (October 1971), 847-859.

Reports findings of study in Israel on the various appeals clients make to influence bureaucrats in their favor. Designed to assess popular orientations to complex organizations. Data derived from content analysis of letters to Israeli customs authorities. Concludes that there is considerable room for personal persuasion and bargaining even within a Weberian bureaucracy.

607. Danet, Brenda and Harriet Hartman. "Coping with Bureaucracy: The Israeli Case." *Social Forces*, 51, 1 (1972), 7-22.

Reports results of survey of attitudes of Israeli citizens toward government in general and bureaucracy in particular. Seeks to test hypotheses regarding (1) correlation of attitudinal competence; (2) the effects of contacts with officials; and (3) the effects of (1) and (2) on coping behavior. Finds that people with little education from Mideastern or North African backgrounds, where bureaucratic norms are weak, are less competent than others. However, actual experience with Israeli bureaucracy serves as a mediating factor.

608. Danet, Brenda and Harriet Hartman. "On 'Proteksia': Orientations Toward the Use of Personal Influence in Israeli Bureaucracy." *Journal of Comparative Administration*, 3, 4 (February 1972), 405-434.

Although Israel has acquired the shell of Western bureaucracy, a system of personal influence--"proteksia"--remains strong. Study based on random sample of 1885 adults in Tel Aviv, Haifa, Jerusalem and Beer Sheba. Finds

that while "bureaucratic" norms are strong,
"nonbureaucratic" behavior predominates.
Most people think that proteksia is widespread
--and useful.

609. Eldersveld, Samuel, V. Jagannadham and A.P.
Barnabas. *The Citizen and The Administra-
tor in a Developing Democracy.* Chicago:
Scott, Foresman, 1968.

Administration for development will not
succeed unless citizens are involved and
mobilized. Presents findings from empirical
study in Delhi state, India, of citizen-
administrator relationships and attitudes.
Based on a stratified random sample of 700
adult citizens and 220 administrators. Finds
high level of bureaucratic penetration,
although there are important educational and
income differentials. Includes appendices
on sample construction and questionnaires.

*   Esman, Milton. *Administration and Development
in Malaysia: Institutions and Reform in a
Plural Society.* Cited as item 484.

610. Friedmann, Karl A. "The Public and the
Ombudsman: Perceptions and Attitudes in
Britain and Alberta." *Canadian Journal of
Political Science,* 10, 3 (September 1977),
497-525.

Empirical assessment of the public's knowledge and appreciation of the ombudsman. Based
on two surveys of the Alberta population and
one survey of the British population. Finds
that knowledge is comparable, although those
who are poor and ill-educated are less aware
of the ombudsman. To equalize access,
targeted information campaigns are needed.

611. Gellhorn, Walter. *Ombudsmen and Others:
     Citizens' Protectors in Nine Countries.*
     Cambridge: Harvard University Press, 1966.

     Describes the structure and operation of
     ombudsmen offices in Denmark, Finland, New
     Zealand, Norway, Sweden, Yugoslavia, Poland,
     the Soviet Union, and Japan. Little compara-
     tive analysis attempted. Concludes that
     while ombudsmen can be effective as grievance-
     handling devices, they are no better than the
     people who occupy the offices.

612. Gregory, Roy and Peter Hutchesson. *The
     Parliamentary Ombudsman: A Study in the
     Control of Administrative Action.* London:
     George Allen and Unwin, 1975.

     Describes the scope and operation of the
     Office of Parliamentary Commissioner in Great
     Britain. Notes that this is similar to but
     still distinct from Scandinavian-style
     ombudsman. Includes a large number of case
     histories. Concludes that while some improve-
     ments can be made in its operation, overall
     the Commissioner scheme has proved very
     effective, and has helped cement parliamentary
     control of administration.

613. Hadi, M.A. "L'Extension de l'Ombudsman:
     Triomphe d'une Idée on Deformation d'une
     Institution?" *International Review of
     Administrative Sciences,* 43, 4 (1977),
     334-344.

     Only in Sweden and Finland have institutions
     true to the original concept of ombudsman been
     developed and maintained. In all other coun-
     tries, the institution has been weakened and
     distorted.

614. Hill, Larry B. "Institutionalization, the
     Ombudsman, and Bureaucracy." *American
     Political Science Review,* 68, 3 (September

1974), 1075-1085.

Focuses on ombudsman-environment interactions in attempt to explain successful institutionalization. Data principally drawn from fieldwork in New Zealand, though some comparisons with Scandinavia, Britain, and U.S. institutions are made. Finds that the office has in fact performed its mission and has established itself with bureaucratic actors as an authority figure.

615. Hill, Larry B. *The Model Ombudsman.* Princeton: Princeton University Press, 1976.

Evaluates twelve and a half years of operation of the Office of Ombudsman in New Zealand, from 1962 to 1975. Begins with theoretical discussion of democracy, bureaucracy and the ombudsman. Describes nature of complaints, characteristics of clients, methods the office uses to process grievances, and effectiveness. Also examines relationships between ombudsman and other political actors.

616. Hill, Michael. *The State, Administration and the Individual.* Totowa, New Jersey: Rowman and Littlefield, 1976.

Theoretical treatment of the relationship between the citizen and the administrative state. Focuses on Great Britain, with a major emphasis on social administration. Treats both how state seeks to control and assist citizenry and how citizenry can and should control administration. Concludes with an assessment of the Skeffington Report, which suggested ways local authorities could involve people in planning.

* Montgomery, John D. *Technology and Civic Life: Making and Implementing Development Decisions.* Cited as item 511.

617. Mossuz-Lavau, Janine. "L'Attitude des Jeunes
     à l'Égard de l'Administration." *International Review of Administrative Sciences*,
     41, 1 (1975), 16-28.

     Reports survey of 470 French youth, aged
     16-34 years, on attitudes toward French
     administration. Finds that most young people
     have a positive view of French public ser-
     vice, believing that any complaints about
     bureaucracy they may have will be fairly
     addressed, and that the civil service is
     oriented toward the "general interest." Also
     analyzes the negative views expressed by a
     minority of respondents and offers explana-
     tions for their attitudes.

618. Nachmias, David and David H. Rosenbloom.
     Bureaucratic Culture. New York: St.
     Martin's Press, 1978.

     Examines the consequences of bureaucratiza-
     tion on the attitudes of citizens and bureau-
     crats in Israeli. Finds distinct patterns
     of reactions to the bureaucratization of
     public life among citizens and between citi-
     zens and bureaucrats. Argues that tension
     between bureaucracy and democracy should be
     reduced. Strategies to accomplish this in-
     clude social representation and participatory
     decision-making.

619. Nagler, Neville. "The Image of the Civil
     Service in Britain." *Public Administration*
     (London), 57 (1979), 127-142.

     Beginning with the assertion that the public
     image of the British Civil Service has eroded
     markedly in the past twenty years, presents
     some reasons for the decline: increased scope
     of governmental activity, expertise of
     administrators, perceived inefficiency, and
     the tendency of politicians to blame bureau-
     crats for their own failings.

620. Nunes, F.E. "The Declining Status of the
Jamaican Civil Service." *Social and
Economic Studies*, 23, 2 (June 1974), 344-
357.

The status of the Jamaican Civil Service
has declined steadily since the 1940's. Provides data comparing with other occupations.
Several explanations for this decline are
considered. Argues that the status erosion
will create serious problems for Jamaica. It
will find it increasingly difficult to attract
and hold administrators, and to achieve com-
pliance with programs.

* Poitras, Guy E. "Welfare Bureaucracy and
Clientele Politics in Mexico." Cited as
Item 302.

621. Pugh, Idwal Sir. "The Ombudsman--Jurisdiction,
Powers, and Practice." *Public Administration* (London), 56 (Summer 1978), 127-138.

Article by the Parliamentary Commissioner
for Administration outlines the operation of
his office. Argues that it has been a substantial success and has helped forge healthier
attitudes in departments toward citizens.
Includes tabular analysis of complaints.

622. Rowat, D.C. "The New Ombudsman Plans in
Western Europe." *International Review of
Administrative Sciences*, 46, 2 (1980), 135-
145.

Discusses recent adoptions of ombudsmen
systems in Italian regional governments, the
Swiss canton of Zurich, and by Portugal and
Austria.

623. Rowat, Donald C. *The Ombudsman Plan: Essays
on the World Wide Spread of an Idea.*
Toronto: Stewart and McCleland, 1973.

Compilation of previous Rowat writings on ombudsmen. Text itself includes historical analysis of ombusmen development, treatment of technical and administrative issues in operation, and case studies of ombudsmen around the world. Extensive appendices include reviews of literature on subject as well as an in-depth bibliography.

*   Samoff, Joel. "The Bureaucracy and the Bourgeoisie: Decentralization and Class Structure in Tanzania." Cited as item 528.

624. Schmidt, Steffen W. "Bureaucrats as Modernizing Brokers? Clientelism in Colombia." *Comparative Politics*, 6, 3 (April 1974), 425-450.

Colombian politics have traditionally been clientelistic. However, the Colombian bureaucracy has increasingly become modernized and technocratic, and less tied to the patronage system of the major political parties. In recent years, the bureaucracy has emerged as a direct broker with clients and has eschewed initiatives from politicians.

625. Stacey, Frank. *Ombudsmen Compared*. Oxford: Clarendon Press, 1978.

Case analyses of origins and functions of ombudsmen in Sweden, Denmark, Norway, Canada, France, and the United Kingdom. Some comparative analysis in concluding chapter, although main emphasis is on single case, discrete treatments.

626. Tomsova, Iva and Atvis Sojka. "L'Action des Administrés sur le Fonctionnement de l'Administration Publique en Tchécoslovaquie." *International Review of Administrative Sciences*, 32, 1 (1966), 33-42.

Argues that Czechs do not merely influence
their administration, but that they, as citizens, actually manage it.   A great deal of
citizen control is exercised through elected
committees at national, regional, and local
levels.

627. Uppendahl, Herbert. "The Ombudsman of
Rheinland-Pfalz: Achievements and Deficiencies." Public Administration (London),
57 (Summer 1979), 219-228.

Reviews the development and operation of the
Office of Ombudsman (Burgerbeauftragter) in
the West German state of Rhineland-Pfalz.
Provides data on number, type and disposition
of complaints processed. Concludes that a
"promising start" has been made.

628. Weeks, Kent M. Ombudsmen Around the World:
A Comparative Chart, 2nd. Ed. Berkeley:
Univeristy of California Press, 1978.

Text consists of data describing the
characteristics of ombudsmen in fourteen countries and twenty-five states or provinces.

PART III

INDICES

Author Index

COUNTRY INDEX